FAITH
& THE
COMMON
GOOD

FAITH & THE COMMON GOOD

The Best of *Zion's Herald*
and *The Progressive Christian*,
2000-2011

STEPHEN SWECKER
Editor

RIDER GREEN BOOK PUBLISHERS

PUBLISHER CERTIFIED
• Limited Edition •
COPY # 76   of 99

The articles reprinted in this volume are used by permission.
Cover Art: "Two Egrets"©Roderick MacIver Arts. Used by permission.

North Berwick ME 03906

Copyright © 2014 Rider Green
All rights reserved.
ISBN-10: 0-9819921-5-3
ISBN-13: 978-0-9819921-5-0
Library of Congress Control Number: 2012946410

DEDICATION

This book is dedicated to the countless faithful readers of *Zion's Herald* and *The Progressive Christian* since the first issue in 1823 until the final press run in 2011, and to the talented writers, designers and editors who kept it relevant and lively for the better part of two centuries.

TABLE OF CONTENTS

Foreword xi
Editor's Preface xviii

ESSAYS   1

Storytelling And Political Leadership 3
    by Eric Mount

Mapping The Human Situation In The Age Of Biotechnology 12
    by Colin B. Gracey

What, Really, Is Patriotism? 17
    by Betty Benner

VIEWPOINT   21

Easy To Hate? 23
    by Donna Schaper

God's Hit Men 25
    by G. Jeffrey MacDonald

One Family's Values 31
    by James Armstrong

UMC Needs A "Third Way" To Heal Itself 36
    by Cynthia B. Astle

The Knife 42
    by Robert Shetterly

At War With Pleasure 46
    by Beverly Dale

Purveyors Of False Memory 54
    by Thom White Wolf Fassett

Confronting Our Fears 60
    by Stephen W. Rankin

Blessing Same-Sex Unions 67
    by Randall Tremba

Creative Intentions 72
    by John Lane Denson

PERSPECTIVE   75

The Hardening Of America 77
    by J. Philip Wogaman

Procedural Justice And Biblical Justice 82
    by Heidi Hadsell

Titanic Christianity 87
    by Steven Blackburn

Ronald Reagan: A Reassessment 92
    by J. Philip Wogaman

Muslims As Partners In Interfaith Encounter 95
    by Jane I. Smith

On And On 101
    by Scott Campbell

Sharing Sacred History And Geography 104
    by Yehezkel Landau

The Offense Of Love 111
    by Scott Campbell

The Strange Case Of Timothy McVeigh 115
    by J. Philip Wogaman

Experiencing Tragedy, Deepening Compassion 118
    by Scott Campbell

Class Struggle And Religion 122
    by Joerg Rieger

POETRY   125

Only Through Your Love We Can Survive 127
    by Ibrahim M. Abu-Rabi'

'Mocracy 129
    by Brian Wren

In The Time Of The Tumult Of Nations 130
    by Samuel Hazo

Your Breath Upon Me 133
    by Lyman Randall

Tour Seven 134
    by Mary Kennan Herbert

Doing The Truth 136
    by Richard M. Gray

REFLECTION   139

The Offering 141
    by Anne Robertson

A Friend Goes To Iraq To Witness For Peace 147
    by Cynthia B. Astle

Preaching To The Easter-Only Crowd 149
    by Donna Schaper

We Would Have Trusted Him With The World 152
    by Jennifer Latham

Creating A Future Worthy Of Our Past 157
    by Lovett H. Weems, Jr.

New Consciousness 162
    by Thomas Ambrogi

On Marriage 167
    by Robert Cummings Neville

The Rediscovery Of Vocation 174
    by Jan Shoemaker

On Not Sharing Our Keys 181
    by Cynthia B. Astle

Remembering Scotty 184
    by Lyman Randall

Coffinisms: A Tribute 187
    by Stephen J. Sidorak, Jr.

REVIEWS   193

You Can't Play The Blues If You Ain't Paid Your Dues 195
    by John Winn

The Nazification Of Islam 200
    by David Shasha

Digging For Zion Beneath The Surface 206
    by Glen Slater

Why Religion Matters 210
    by Dennis Patrick Slattery

When Life Calls Out To Us 214
    by William B. Gould

SHORT TAKES   217

Renaming The Apocalypse 219
    by Joe Bageant

Survival Of The Fattest 222
    by Charles Schuster

Cole Porter And The Middle East 225
    by John Lovelace

FAITHWRITER   227

Of Moose and Men 229

Jesus Saves 232

Oyster Ethics 235

Gimme Cod 238

SPECIAL REPORT   241

Follow The Money 243
    by Andrew J. Weaver and Nicole Seibert

AUTHORS   259

Index Of Authors   261

FOREWORD

IN 1823 THE METHODIST CHURCH as an organized denomination in the United States was just two years shy of its 40th birthday. The United States itself was less than 50 years old as a nation. There were an estimated 1 billion souls on Earth as compared to over 7 billion in 2012. James Monroe was the fifth President of the United States, and with his Monroe Doctrine warned the world to keep its hands off North America or be prepared for war! There were only 24 stars on the flag of the United States; less than half of our states were a part of the country as we know it today.

Methodism as a worldwide movement (today about 80 million) was hardly begun, but along the eastern seaboard of the United States and with westward expansion of the fledgling country, it was riding the tide of what in historical circles is called the "Second Great Awakening." Theologically, classical Arminianism (humankind is born in depravity but God has gifted each person with "free will" to climb to holiness and spiritual salvation) and Wesleyan Arminianism (John Wesley's combining of free will with humankind's ability to move toward a more perfect life) had been a force in the movement from colonial America to the establishment of the United States. It is a small step in most minds from "I am free to make choices leading to my own salvation" to "why am I not therefore free to make choices leading to my own governance?" And the doctrine of going on to spiritual perfection (not totally, but more perfectly as one works toward it) lends itself nicely to both national manifest destiny and personal achievement of a better life through hard work, otherwise known as the Protestant work ethic.

So, in the early 1800s, Methodist circuit riders moved throughout the ever-expanding towns and villages of the growing nation, preaching a message of hope and an ethic of promise. Hard work, physical and spiritual, was to be rewarded with a better life – now and in the hereafter!

Any growing social movement requires a public voice and a way of communicating within its circle of influence. In 1823 Zion's Herald became the first such voice within the Methodist movement in the United States. Founded and published in Boston, it quickly became the medium for the message as the Methodist movement spread out across the country, and it remained that for almost 200 years. It was at times merely a house organ. At other junctures, however, it was a clear and prophetic voice within the Methodist Church and many other like-minded denominations as well.

For most of its history, *Zion's Herald* has been a voice for the progressive tendencies in the Methodist movement. These have included abolitionism, women's suffrage, prohibition (once considered a progressive concern), the rise of the labor movement, segregation, civil rights, feminism, environmental sustainability, economic justice and, most recently, justice in same-sex marriage and ordination.

The format of the publication for a long period in its life was a tabloid-sized weekly. Various editors set the tone from their own style and interests. In general, there was a rather eclectic lineup of news from around the religious and secular world, including the most prominent stories of the past week. But, the unique religious flavor came from sermons, standing features on Sunday school programming, regular articles on the women's organizations in the New England church, letters to the editor, advertisements from merchants in the northeast, and editorial commentary on the hot button issues of the day. This was interspersed with personal greetings around birthdays and anniversaries, news of local church celebrations and appeals for funds in support of various mission and denominational activities.

Zion's Herald went through a succession of name changes. Most were inconsequential and did not last long. One editor, a staunch traditionalist, sought to counter the rising movement in the church for gender-free and inclusive language by renaming it *The Churchman*. That rather passive-aggressive dalliance was reversed by the publishers within a matter of a year or two amidst a swell of voices from feminist readers who dropped subscriptions rapidly.

Reading old issues gives a wonderful and sometimes very amusing glimpse into religious thought and direction over the years. While the publication itself tended to lean toward either progressive views or to stay neutral and let the readership propound their inclinations, one still gets a wide view of the discussions of any particular era. Early in the 1900s, before the outbreak of World War I, the churches (and especially women in the church) were deeply immersed in the issues of temperance and suffrage. The leadership roster on these issues leading up to the enactment of the 18th amendment (granting women the right to vote) and the 19th amendment (establishing prohibition) shortly after the close of the First World War is replete with women leading the charge. Sadly, what is lost in much of today's concerns for equal pay and professional opportunities for women, and for violence against women, is that these issues are on a continuum that runs through our society dating from the prohibition and suffrage movements. Women have been moving us forward as a society for most of the 20th century!

But, during the opening years of the 20th century, the argument among men, especially clergy, against the suffrage movement was that it took women's energy away from the temperance efforts. The Reverend W. S. Matthew wrote a letter to the editor published in 1912 to support a previous letter that avowed "no state has adopted woman suffrage without setting back the temperance cause twenty-five years." Mr. Matthew went on to write:

"I am led to say it seems to me too early to decide what will be the final effect of woman suffrage upon the cause of temperance and other great reform movements. Personally, I, with multitudes of other sincere men, had always opposed woman suffrage on the ground that woman already has burdens sufficient, and that she cannot be spared from the noblest work ever to be committed to her hands and heart, the rearing of children and the care of the home."

Sadly, that refrain is still sung today when we speak of the role of women in our life and world.

A sampling of the headline stories from 1923 provides a glimpse into the variety of issues reported and discussed in the years following World War I. In an April, 1923 issue, the editor presented detailed discussions on the agreement reached by the United States government with Finland to repay the latter's debts to the U.S. following the Great War, a detailed discussion on whether or not recent astronomical observations finally did or did not confirm Einstein's Theory of Relativity and a lengthy exploration of the problems of child labor in the beet fields of Colorado and Michigan. Other topics during that period range from interpreting scenes in "Othello," to "An Inside View of the Situation in the Ruhr" by an Army officer who represented the United States on the Rhineland Commission, to an exploration of whether immigrant workers in the United States are truly "Human Beings or Cogs in a Machine?" The later was subtitled "A Constructive Approach to the Problem of the Alien in Our Midst." Sound familiar?

Throughout much of its history *Zion's Herald* and *The Progressive Christian* (as it was re-named in 2007) strove to draw upon the wisdom and insight of its readership for articles and opinions. And the readership at any given point in the long history of these publications contained some of the most prominent voices of the day. There were scientists and statesmen, preachers and politicians. It published sermons by some of the great voices of the day including Harry Emerson Fosdick and Ralph Sockman. Few remember them now, but in the mid-20th century they were the pulpit equivalents of the media preachers of our generation, *sans* the faux personas and money grubbing!

In the issue published just days following the Pearl Harbor attack (just a few weeks before Christmas), the editor asked a number of prominent preachers: "Now that we are at war, what will you say in your pulpits this Christmas season?" Most, in some form or another, said they would stick with the traditional Christmas story since it was about hope and promise as much as anything else they might lean on.

At many critical moments in the history of the United States and Methodism in particular, the pages of *Zion's Herald* and *The Progressive Christian* have offered the Christian community a clear and unequivocal sense of direction. As clearly as we see the issues leading up to World War II today, they were not so black and white at the outset of that war. Many prominent Americans, including Henry Ford and Charles Lindberg, believed that Hitler and the Axis had much to offer in an emerging industrial world. They, of course, were sadly misled. L. O. Hartman, long-time editor of *Zion's Herald*, made it very clear from the outset of our participation in that war that we were dealing with morally "treacherous" and dangerous Axis leaders. He wrote:

"We are at war. In the midst of peaceful negotiations, the Japanese, without a declaration of war, suddenly on Sunday attacked our naval bases at Honolulu and other points in the Pacific. Under the stress of superheated emotions, Americans will now be thinking mainly of the physical conflict that is to ensue, and of the hoped-for victory of our forces. But there is an inner meaning to the incidents of Sunday that we should not miss. It takes us into the deeper ranges of theology, religion and ethics. We face the might of a violent paganism that would reduce to a dead materialism all that we have been taught to regard as "sweetness and light"... It is sad indeed to have to say it, but we are now fighting for our lives, yes, for the very existence of the fruits of civilization and for those ethical imperatives without which civilization is impossible."

The role of religious journalism has always been to call us to the truth – and to our personal and communal highest and best!

Publishing *Zion's Herald* and *The Progressive Christian* was always an expensive proposition. Subscriptions and advertisements alone were never sufficient to keep the enterprise afloat. Through most of the 20th century the newspaper was owned and published by the Boston Wesleyan Association. The Association owned several key pieces of downtown Boston real estate, and the income from those office buildings supplemented the costs of the paper. When those properties were sold, the income from the residual assets was still not wholly able to continue the publication. To make ends meet in the later years of the century, the Association shared its editorial and publishing office staff with the Boston Area of The United Methodist Church in several joint ventures. At various times, the editor was also the Chaplain/Executive Director of the New England Social and Industrial Relations Committee (United Methodist). This work included a presence on many ecumenical bodies, labor union ministries and social justice committees.

At one point or another the editor of Zion's Herald was also working on concerns and with groups addressing the church's ministry around issues like racism in labor unions, Project Equality, persons enduring hardships due to prolonged strikes, The United Farm Workers Union, native American unemployment issues, governmental policies on collective bargaining, prison ministries and helping local churches set up employment hot lines. Consistent with its more prophetic stances, the editors dealt with such divisive issues as advocating for pardons for Viet Nam War draft dodgers and re-establishing diplomatic and economic ties with the government of Cuba.

THIS VOLUME GIVES GOOD INSIGHT into the historical period (first decade of the 21st century) of *Zion's Herald* and *The Progressive Christian*. Under the editorial leadership of Stephen Swecker and, later, Cynthia Astle, the journalism reflected in *The Progressive Christian* reached its peak. Good and perceptive authors, timely material on issues of the day and skilled editorial work produced a final decade of award-winning publications. The rising tides of a preemptive war mentality nurtured by the "neocon" politics of the last decade coupled with right-wing reactionary religious conservatism, a new "greed" mentality of the super-rich and crumbling economics of the middle class has led to a culture of fear among millions of Americans. Popular media religious figures have exploited this with the hollow promises of their "prosperity gospels." But the real and legitimate work of supportive community is still being done by faithful local congregations in an uphill battle to help create and sustain meaningful and hopeful journeys through life. There has been much to address, and *The Progressive Christian* rose to that task right up to its last issue in 2011.

But religious journalism now finds itself in a unique setting in the world of mass communications. It has been set upon by a "perfect storm" of change in societal communications. The media is now largely controlled by the vested interests of the military and big business, the "military-industrial complex" against which President Eisenhower warned us. Large segments of so-called journalism are divisive, politically motivated, unfair and unbalanced tools in the hands of special interests. Talk radio and social media have swept historically ethical journalism into the realm of partial truth and innuendo. Print media has been, by its very nature, relegated to the world of yesterday's news before it is even put to paper. The TV screen and the computer monitor have largely replaced books and newspapers. Deep probing and reflective thought has been replaced by sound bites. This is a sad but fast emerging reality, and it threatens the whole spectrum of worldwide journalism that has served society's interest so well for centuries.

Against that background, the 188-year history of *Zion's Herald* and *The Progressive Christian* has been a remarkable journey through and contribution to the interdependent movement of religion and society throughout American history. Religious thought has shaped the American experience, and the American cultural journey has shaped the church. Historian Sidney Mead has called the United States' unique blend of religious freedom and plurality a "lively experiment" in world history; no nation had ever before survived without a state-sanctioned religion. This lively experiment has been an epic journey, and, for nearly 200 years, *Zion's Herald* and *The Progressive Christian* chronicled it all.

Thomas J. Gallen
Executive Director
The Preachers' Aid Society of New England

EDITOR'S PREFACE

THIS VOLUME REFLECTS THE ECLECTIC CHARACTER of the publication from which its contents have been compiled. Since its founding in 1823, *Zion's Herald* (re-named *The Progressive Christian* in 2007) published a remarkable array of editorial content. Church-related news was always its anchor, initially as an independent publication in its earliest days but later as an extension of New England Methodism for most of its amazingly long history. Interspersed with its ecclesiastical reporting, particularly during the 19th century, were such items as news about ships currently docked in Boston's harbor, their expected arrival and departure dates, the price of dry goods, financial news, and scuttlebutt about New England's social leaders, religious and otherwise. Its advertising in those days reflected this eclecticism as well, much of it having no discernible relationship whatsoever to the church or religion!

    The one trait that gave it a distinctive focus across the years, however, was a general dissatisfaction with the *status quo* and openness to new developments in the church and society, i.e., to progress. Today we would call such an open, inquiring and challenging stance toward the world and religion "progressive" – not knee-jerk "liberal" in the current ideological sense of the word, but never reactionary or averse to "making waves." Mostly, though, it was forward-looking with the optimism of a religious worldview shaped by respect for factual reporting and a passion for Christian social justice.

What follows in these pages is a compilation of pieces selected from 2000-2011, the final dozen years of the publication's long history. No effort has been made to identify themes or organize the material by subject matter. Rather, using section headings that correspond generally to headings used in the magazine during this era, the pieces included here are samples from the publication during this time frame: a little bit of this, a little bit of that, all reflective of the progressive and socially forward-looking spirit of its readers, contributors and editors.

As one would expect of material compiled from a periodical, some pieces in this collection clearly are dated, i.e., expressions of the particular historical context of the first decade of the 21st century. Others, however, sound as relevant as when they were first published. Taken as a whole, therefore, the collection serves as something of a benchmark for how far we've come, or have not come, in relationship to matters we regarded as important in that eventful decade.

Are the items selected for publication here unarguably the "best" material to be found in the magazine during this era? Of course not. The most that we can say is that they represent the wide range of high-quality contributions published over a twelve-year period, far more than could be packed into a single reasonably sized volume. For this reason, it was both easy and difficult to make the final selections for inclusion. In the end, we've done our best to serve up a taste of the magazine's rich diversity based on a range of factors, including subject matter, authorship, length and so on.

What's missing is regrettable but unavoidable: the physical beauty of the actual magazine during its final dozen years as a product of gifted and creative contributors, editors, artists and technicians. All of those who lifted *Zion's Herald* and *The Progressive Christian* to new heights during this time took great pride in their work and garnered a wall's worth of national awards for their efforts. In gratitude, we salute them.

— **Stephen Swecker**

STORYTELLING AND POLITICAL LEADERSHIP
Eric Mount (2008)

"Perhaps no other culture so clearly defines itself by its morality tales."
– Robert Reich, *Tales of a New America*

ELECTION CYCLES IN OUR SOCIETY typically involve the retelling of our nation's stories and the proposal of revised or even new narratives with which to identify ourselves. The American Dream, the City on a Hill, the New Frontier, the Great Society, the Bridge to the Twenty- first Century, the Fair Deal, the New Deal, the War on Poverty, the Reagan Revolution, and numerous other mottos have summoned us either to our roots or to a new identity as a people.

Because of the security they give us, it is not easy to abandon or modify the traditional stories and learn to tell new ones about ourselves. But what if a changed world calls for changed stories? That we live in such a world that calls for such a change was precisely the claim of award-winning Clinton administration labor secretary Robert R. Reich when he wrote *Tales of a New America* in 1987.

Reich, then a Harvard political economist and now professor of public policy at the University of California at Berkeley, believed that our most cherished stories or "morality tales" had outlived their usefulness in their traditional forms. We needed, he argued, to learn to tell better stories about ourselves in a shrinking, increasingly interdependent world. However valid and useful the stories had been in the past, the four major American morality tales needed to change because they all pitted "us" against "them" both domestically and globally, even if they sometimes envisioned "us" doing good things for "them" rather than "us" disciplining or defeating "them." Two decades later it is apparent that we haven't heeded his admonition, and his more recent writings, such as *The Future of Success* (2000) and *Supercapitalism* (2007), don't suggest otherwise.

Meanwhile, the need for better stories has probably grown as new developments have accelerated the trends he cited at the same time that commitment has hardened to the four traditional morality tales that Reich considered outdated. Will this election cycle convince us of the need for better stories (and what is better is admittedly a judgment call), or will it prompt a re-enforcement of our entrenchment in those four revered tales? It will take compelling leadership to sell a narrative more adequate to today's challenges.

Telling the four tales

The four tales that Reich saw woven in our history and espoused by conservatives and liberals alike, often in differing renditions and combinations, are the Mob at the Gates (about foreigners), the Triumphant Individual (about entrepreneurs and workers), the Benevolent Community (about the poor), and the Rot at the Top (about big business and big government). How do these tales frame the way we look at issues?

About "the Mob," conservatives and liberals have not always identified the same "dark forces" (Reich's term) that threaten the order and security of our society or advocated the same strategies toward them, but we all have our mobs. Nazi Germany and Japan at the time of World War II, the Soviet threat, "the Yellow Peril," Japanese auto imports, international drug traffic, terrorists, illegal immigrants (at times all immigrants), and other nations that are unreliable allies or unfair competitors are a good start on a list.

Reich was quick to acknowledge that there is evil abroad in the world, but in an interdependent world that survived the Iron Curtain and the nuclear arms race (so far) and has seen the development of the Japanese-American corporation, he questioned neat divisions of the world into "the evil others" and "the good Americans." He even stated, "But there is no mob. And there are no gates" (p. 102). In other words, the international drug traffic is not only a Columbian problem; it is also an American problem.

The tale of the Triumphant Individual exalts the ingenuity of the entrepreneur who succeeds by dint of individual initiative and hard work. The flip side can be that poverty is an insult to the victim and in no way a problem for the successful. In a world of winners and losers, you pick your team. Our history has seen numerous heroic examples of realizing the American Dream, but our individualist myth can overlook the indebtedness of the successful to others, the prevalence of triumphant teams (such as group winners of Nobel Prizes), and the undeserved barriers to prosperity that the poor experience. Reich saw the times of the Great Depression and World War II as a period when Americans felt a large measure of solidarity with their fellow citizens and thought more in terms of "our" problems than of theirs and mine. In his view, we have seldom seen such solidarity since.

The Benevolent Community story of barn-raisings and United Ways has never disappeared from our society, and Reich cited religious communities as having, from early in our history, influenced our national sense of community to be more inclusive, advocating full rights of community membership for slaves and women, for example. With such social programs as the War on Poverty, however, we have been better at charitable efforts by "us" for "them" than we have been at concerted efforts to address problems viewed as affecting us all. For conservatives, the marginalized may need discipline, and for liberals they may need relief, but both have "us" doing what is best for "them" instead of affirming a sense of shared membership in a national community or a global community.

The fourth morality tale, the Rot at the Top, may locate the problem in big government or big business, but Americans have had a nose for the corruption of power from our start. Unchecked power does corrupt, and Reich's more recent Supercapitalism cites the "not quite Golden Age" (the three decades after World War II) when big business, big government and big labor had a balance of power that saw us through. Now, he laments, the global economy has advanced the interests of the consumer and the investor at the expense of the concern for the common good that should characterize civic virtue of the citizenry in a democracy. Instead, profits are equated with the common good.

When Reich wrote *Tales of a New America*, he was concerned about a too- facile location of all rot in one sector of our national life, whether in Washington or the corporate boardroom. As he observed, "Americans are determined to take their devils one at a time." Instead he advocated being vigilant about rot wherever it exists and appreciative of the varied roles that business and government have to play for the general welfare or the common good. Once again, he saw a crying need for stories that recognized social solidarity and interdependence amid the overlapping interests of increased globalization.

Entrenched or transcendent?

In the two decades since his challenge to tell better stories about ourselves, plenty has happened that could either entrench us more deeply in the old stories or spur us to stories that transcend the "us" against "them" liability of the four traditional tales. In the current political campaign, the candidates have seemed more concerned with "the vision thing" than their recent predecessors, and they are trying in differing ways to appeal to a desire for change in the electorate, as evidenced in polling statistics about satisfaction with the current administration. At the same time, they have invoked some of the standard themes of the four venerable morality tales (the American Dream, for example). What may distinguish them from each other is the extent to which they attempt to lead us to tell better stories about ourselves that expand the reach of our sense of solidarity and move us beyond "us" and "them" polarities and divisions both domestically and globally. How well can they engage us in a common search for a common good?

The Mob at the Gates has certainly not disappeared from our political rhetoric. The dark outside forces that threaten our homeland security have forged their way into even greater prominence since 9/11. The "clash of civilizations", the growing numbers of terrorists, the greater influx of illegal immigrants, the former allies who have not joined us in Iraq, and varied religious (read "Muslim"), racial, and ethnic "others" are variously identified as threats to our security.

In a recent column entitled "Getting Bubba," Kathleen Parker observes this about a portion of the American electorate that fears the loss of our nation's heritage and traditional values amid our burgeoning diversity and pluralism: "What they sense is that their heritage is being swept under the carpet while multiculturalism becomes the new national narrative. And they fear what else might be lost in the remodeling of America" (The Advocate-Messenger, May 15, 2008, p. A9). What some would propose as a better story about ourselves, a multicultural narrative, is seen only as a threat (a mob) to these Americans. For some the lament about lost heritage can be a conscious or unconscious cover for racism, but for others it can have a more commendable rationale.

Two decades deeper into globalization, the new economic giants—China, India, and Brazil—may also seem like new mobs and new threats to America's long- enjoyed pre-eminence and hegemony. In Fareed Zakaria's words, "We have become suspicious of trade, openness, immigration, and investment because now it's not Americans going abroad but foreigners coming to America. Just as the world is opening up, we are closing down." ("The Post-American World," *Newsweek*, May 12, 2008, 31)

In our culture wars, people with "other" sexual orientations are perceived by some as a threat to the institution of marriage and to the foundations of our civilization. Through gated communities, withdrawal to new homogeneous communities removed from mixed neighborhoods, and other residential and educational "sorting mechanisms" (a Reich term from *The Future of Success*, now echoed in

Bill Bishop's *The Big Sort*), many Americans seek to insulate themselves from increasingly pervasive pluralism and multiculturalism. Efforts to expand the circle of "we," to find common ground, to discover overlapping interests, to seek common cause with the "others" persist, but they have an uphill climb to make.

A persistent belief

Meanwhile, our unabated individualism supports a persistent belief that we need not concern ourselves about the common good. It will allegedly take care of itself if we all continue to pursue our own self-interest without stultification by governmental regulation. As Reich further argues in The Future of Success, the decline of institutional loyalty has produced the reduction of careers to a series of contracts, the reduction of community to a commodity instead of a sense of belonging, and the reduction of higher education to a way to make contacts more than a way to experience a tradition and prepare for democratic citizenship. Such recent developments as the heightened awareness of the threat of climate change and the spread of concern to an ever-broader constituency provide a pull toward more "commons" sense on behalf of our planet and our progeny, but any suggestion that the relentless push for economic growth should be tempered by environmental stewardship can be a tough sell in some quarters.

What Reich saw as a version of the Benevolent Community morality tale that is outdated, lives on in the desire to reduce the social safety net, rely more on faith-based agencies and private contractors, and shrink the government, in the words of Grover Norquist, leader of Americans for Tax Reform, "to the size where it can be drowned in a bathtub." The Katrina tragedy and ensuing fiasco showed that we still want government to be our friend when disaster of certain kinds strikes and that we feel betrayed when it is not. It has also shown us that the wells of national community spirit have not run dry. The front burner status of proposals for universal health care in the current campaign also suggests a surge of support for government involvement in protecting us from financial ruin due to medical misfortune. (It is noteworthy that neither of the surviving major candidates would frown on an active role for government to near the extent that our current administration does, although they clearly differ on the issue.)

Still fuels discourse

The Rot at the Top morality tale obviously still fuels the discourse of the campaign trail, and with good reasons. Washington, we hear, is where good ideas go to die. Our leaders are charged with having misled us about Iraq. Lobbyists for "special interests" are leading our representatives astray. Enron and World Com head an impressive recent list of corporate malefactors. Oil companies, pharmaceutical companies, no-bid contractors in Iraq, and risky mortgage lenders have ripped us off. Looking abroad we can cite genocidal rulers, governmental blockers and seizers of food aid in crisis situations, and international companies that exploit labor and spoil the environment. There is no indication that corruption of power and disregard of the common good are going out of style. When we look at international talks about controlling emissions and otherwise addressing climate change, what we have often seen is a recycling of "us" against "them" rhetoric by developed and developing countries about each other.

If we take global warming as Exhibit A, we and the other nations of the world are facing a threat to our global commons that jeopardizes all of us, as well as other life forms and future generations. If we are to tell better stories about ourselves and other nations, it would seem that we had best acknowledge that we are all part of the rot and that we need to find common ground among nations and between government and business based on mutual interest, even with those we regard as our adversaries or our enemies. Likewise, the growing gap between the world's rich and the world's poor and the ravages of the AIDS pandemic necessitate more framing of issues as "our problems" rather their "their problems" or "my problems." Still the voices summoning us to tell better stories about ourselves at home and abroad are often considered unrealistic and out of touch. (I did not follow closely what better stories Reich may have tried to sell when he ran for governor in Massachusetts recently, but he fared poorly at the polls.)

Here we are then in what Zakaria is calling "the post-American world" (a term in decided contrast to the "American Empire" narrative that has been both bandied about and roundly criticized of late). This "post-American world" is hard to take as well as hard to take in for many Americans. This world is increasingly globalized and interdependent due to trade, technology, and other problems that do not observe national borders. It is also frightfully fraught with fragmentation and polarization and bloody tribal, ethnic, and religious conflict. Within our own nation, we are "red" and "blue" states, we are black and brown and white, and we speak of class wars and culture wars. We are ripe for leadership that will bring us together for some high purpose greater than what is in it for "us" against "them." Columnist Leonard Pitts wrote recently, "No one says 'we' when they talk about homelessness or hunger, no "our" enters the discussion of fatherless families or abortion rights, "us" is a stranger to the debate over failing schools and crime. These conversations are framed by words like 'them' and 'they." ("A hunger for national purpose," The Courier-Journal, April 23, 2008, p. A7)

As Reich pointed out in *Tales of a New America*, our religious communities have at times been major influences in our history that have expanded the inclusiveness of our national community. They have also done some good at expanding narrow nationalism. In our current situation, it is debatable whether religious communities are more part of the problem or of the solution when it comes to building a greater sense of human solidarity in our national and our global communities. Our time sorely needs both religious and political leaders that can help us tell better stories about ourselves, stories that match the realities of a world in crisis, stories that prompt dialogue about the common good.

Language on the trail

Some analysts of campaign rhetoric have observed the relative prominence of "I" language, "they" language, and "we" language among candidates on the campaign trail. They flag an important consideration. Equally important, if not more so, is who is included in "we." If we are as ripe for "change" as the polls indicate, are we ripe for leadership that will dare us to tell better stories about ourselves as Americans? By better, let us hope that we mean stories that move us beyond fruitless antagonisms between "us" and "them" to a solidarity that finds a way to work together for a common good about which people at the bottom as well as the top have a voice.

Social conflict is not going away, and sometimes we may fear "the other" for good reasons. Our fears, however, become self-fulfilling prophecies if we are always acting on our worst suspicions of "the other" instead of seeking areas of overlap between our problems, our interests, and even our hopes. Trying to tell stories that move us beyond the counter-productive antagonisms of "us" against "them will not make all of our differences go away, but better stories could restore a sense of community membership in our land and even beyond our borders that has characterized us in our best moments as a people. In a world of increasingly inescapable interdependence and mutual vulnerability, the need has never been greater.

MAPPING THE HUMAN SITUATION IN THE AGE OF BIOTECHNOLOGY
Colin B. Gracey (2001)

ZION'S HERALD READERS ARE NO DOUBT familiar with James Russell Lowell's well-known hymn, "Once to Every Man and Nation," words from which are still pertinent today:

> ... *new occasions teach new duties,*
> *time makes ancient good uncouth;*
> *They must upward still and onward*
> *who would keep abreast of truth.*

The recent announcement of the mapping of the human genome represents a significant "new occasion" as we move into what may be called the "Age of Biotechnology." This period of creativity probably will be marked as having begun with the first description of the structure of DNA in 1953. Growth in genetic and biotechnology has burgeoned since then. The result has raised interesting new questions and challenges, particularly regarding the integration of that growth with existing life processes.

One such challenge will be to garner the exciting breakthroughs of scientific creativity, to assess their importance, and then to balance their possibilities with complex human and societal needs. This challenge will require insight and wisdom so that growth can be integrated and allowed to proceed in a sustainable manner.

Fortunately, while scientists have been busy with genetic research and technological developments, including the mapping of the human genome, others have been mapping the human situation in which all this is taking place. Part of this work has been federally financed by the Human Genome Project itself. However, much of the mapping of the human situation is being done by independent, non-profit/non-governmental organizations. These organizations are raising issues of concern about the social, ethical, legal and environmental implications of the new genetic technologies. Their work helps to foster discussion, dialogue and debate about the impact of this creativity upon the existing human situation and vice versa.

The contributions of these organizations are as important as the scientific developments themselves because in the end, they can have a significant impact upon the human situation and the world. Equally, people involved with the scientific and technological developments are very much part of the dialogue involved in mapping the human situation. Their technical findings in many cases help clarify issues that must be considered in any such mapping.

The Council for Responsible Genetics is an independent, non-profit and non-governmental organization based in Cambridge, Mass. Founded in 1983, the Council has been working towards the responsible development of genetic technology. Among its recent projects has been to map the human situation based on values that have served the human community well. These are values that may be affected both positively and negatively by developments in genetic technologies. Such potential effects on values lie at the heart of the challenge to integrate our common life with developments in the life sciences.

At one level, mapping the human situation raises the question: "How can we benefit from what biotechnology and genetic technology may offer us and avoid the abuses and negative side-effects these same technologies may cause?" At another level it asks the question: "What values within the human situation and the world need to be maintained and built upon for a better future?"

Following are the value areas identified by The Council for Responsible Genetics along with my editorial comment.

- We value common life that is free from discrimination. We are not there yet, but it is a value that informs what we regard as a societal and ethical goal. We must not permit forms of genetic discrimination to be added to the burden society already carries with other forms of discrimination.
- We prize the right to privacy. We need to affirm this right by supporting the right of individuals to prevent the taking or storing of bodily samples for genetic information without an individual's explicit and voluntary informed consent.
- We have enjoyed a food supply that has not been genetically engineered and that has had oversight by our Food and Drug Administration (FDA). This oversight function has served us well both in terms of testing the safety and handling of food and in terms of labeling food for nutritional value and manner of processing. Unfortunately, the FDA's view of genetically engineered food to date is problematic and is undermining public confidence in the way it is handling issues of safety and labeling of genetically engineered food.
- We value the integrity of our judicial system even though it is far from perfect. DNA tests need to be made available now for anyone and everyone to defend themselves in criminal proceedings. Circumstances that have arisen in Illinois, which have prompted the governor to temporarily suspend executions, should cause us all to pause. With the help of DNA testing, 13 of 25 persons on death row have been set free because they either were not guilty of the crimes for which they were accused or unfairly tried and found guilty.
- We have long held that living things could not be patented. This changed in a 5 to 4 decision by the U.S. Supreme Court in 1980. Since then the patenting of living organisms, including human

genes, animals, plants, microorganism and their parts has become the rule. Many feel the social destructiveness of the patenting of living things far outweighs its value. The decision to allow the patenting of living things may one day have to be revisited. For economic reasons the patent office has extended intellectual property rights to living entities and set in motion a whole new set of problems.

- We have benefited from and valued the richness of the earth's biological and genetic diversity. It will require work to preserve this valued resource from encroachment in the days ahead.
- All of us benefit from living in healthy environments that are free from toxins, contaminants or actions that might harm our genetic makeup. The value of such unpolluted or undisrupted environments may become seriously undermined by genetic technologies.
- The dreams of eugenic measures to improve the human condition or society have proved to be nightmares more often than not. Eugenics under the name of therapeutic advance or enhancement will be difficult to resist in our highly competitive culture. But the value of hard questioning and genuine skepticism of proposed eugenic measures may serve us well.
- To date we have valued the right of a child to be conceived, gestated and born without genetic manipulation. It is a value we have extended to the yet to be born. It is a gold standard that we may need to work hard to maintain.
- Indigenous people for years have managed their own biological resources. Today they are organizing to preserve their traditional knowledge and to protect what they have developed from expropriation by external scientific, corporate or government interests. The rights of indigenous people need to be respected. Those who would exploit these riches need to be challenged by indigenous and non-indigenous people everywhere.

Zion's Herald readers as Christians, no doubt, are confident that whatever the truth may be with respect to these matters, it will ultimately prevail. However, as Christians, they will have had enough experience in the ways of the world to know that we best proceed with humility and great care as the Age of Biotechnology moves us toward the realities of tomorrow.

Such humility and care will require the active participation of and respect for those who will be affected by proposed changes resulting from genetic research. In social terms, this will require a political process that is in accord with democratic principles. It also will require us who are members of faith communities to take these issues to heart as they bear upon our personal lives, our work and its impact on the world, our life in community, and our openness to God's leading.

Integration of the creative growth offered by genetic and biotechnology is promising, yet dangerous. Nevertheless, creative growth built upon solid science coupled with careful and faithful integration with the life process will prove enormously fruitful. Perhaps the final stanza of James Russell Lowell's hymn realistically foreshadows the road ahead:

Though the cause of evil prosper,
Yet 'tis truth alone is strong;
Though her portion be the scaffold,
And upon the throne be wrong,
Yet that scaffold sways the future,
And, behind the dim unknown,
Standeth God within the shadow
Keeping watch above his own.

WHAT, REALLY, IS PATRIOTISM?

| Something to do with a sense of place – and not losing your parents |

Betty Benner (2006)

EACH MONTH I TRAVEL the 50-some miles from Austin, Minnesota, to Plainview to the Third Wednesday open-mike program of the Rural America Writers Coop. We gather a van full of Austinites and cross the prairie for an evening of reading our own poems, listening to others, drinking coffee and eating cookies. We gather in the foyer of the Jon Hassler Theater, which at one time was an International Harvester dealership. Now it presents good plays and makes a home for writers and poets of all kinds, with workshops and seminars and special events designed to bring out the writer in ordinary people.

Part of the mission of the place is to develop in writers "...individual and collective creative abilities and skills, and to enhance the culture of rural and small town America. To serve as a Center for the rekindling and maintenance of the voice of change in the world perspective based on *agrarian life and values.*" (italics mine)

For Third Wednesday last September, I read a column on patriotism I had written in 2003 for the Austin Post Bulletin. It is as true for me today as it was then. It says what I want to say about what's happening out in the world and what's going on at home, in this country and in this county:

"I've lived in Southern Minnesota all my life. I was born and schooled in Mankato, taught in Waseca and Cleveland, and then came to Austin in the early '50's to settle down and raise three daughters. My attachment to this place, this arc of the globe, is deep.

"I think of Mankato as my hometown, imprinted as I am with a childhood spent along the Minnesota and Blue Earth Rivers. But I have adopted Austin. Or maybe it has adopted me. When my Cottage Grove daughter and granddaughter speak of my moving closer to them, not far from the biggest river yet, my feet become only more firmly planted on the banks of the Cedar.

"My bones have grown accustomed to the Mill Pond walk— its outlook, its history, the rich prairie earth and cornfields surrounding. Even the Hormel Company across the way. When poet Gary Snyder says, 'Stop somewhere!', I smile. I settled in years ago, and hopefully poetry is coming out of that. Austin and I chose one another.

"I think about these things as July 4 nears and the summer wind ruffles the rich green of the boulevard maples and my neighbor trims the corners of his lawn while his daughter plays in the sprinkler.

"Patriotism is on my mind. I try to pin it down. Does it have to do with this sense of place I'm feeling? Southern Minnesota is where I am a part of the sequence of lives, from Danish grandparents to six siblings to daughters disbursed, to grandchildren graduating this year, Kate from college at Eau Claire, Ross from Park High in The Grove.

"Here I have had long association with neighbors who have a certain knowledge in their bones, knowledge that leads to doing good work and living pretty good lives, being committed to the community with their particular skills, and reaching out to community-minded people in nearby towns and cities. Ours are not perfect lives, but a striving for good to pass along, a realization that the necessary work of the world is to take what one has and make one's corner better.

"From beyond this place, another voice for patriotism rolls in. It comes in the official call for us to be militant as a nation. Our National Security Agency strategy defines our conflict for us as 'politically motivated violence perpetrated against innocents.' Says Wendell Berry (Kentucky farmer- writer-poet) in his 'Citizen's Response' to this strategy (Orion magazine for March- April 2003): "The NSA wishes terrorism to be seen in the same light as slavery, piracy, or genocide."

"There is no acknowledgement, Berry states, that terrorism might have a cause that possibly could be discovered and possibly remedied. Berry turns the tables. He feels that the 'legitimate' warfare of technologically advanced nations is itself premeditated, politically motivated violence perpetrated against innocents.

"In another article, 'The Failure of War' (Yes Magazine, Winter 2001-2002), Berry states: 'If you know even as little history as I do, it is hard not to doubt the efficacy of modern war as a solution to any problem except that of retribution—the justice of exchanging one damage for another.'

"In defining my patriotism, I discover that I cannot be stirred for war, or by it. Nor can I be stirred, beyond a decent respect, by flags shown on lapels or windows or bumpers or chancels. My personal patriotism, I suspect, in final analysis, lies in being a part of this place where I live, for as long as I live.

"I will strive to keep it clean, without dirtying some other place. I will work to have the old and young learn from one another. I will be neighborly. I will welcome new faces and lift up those that have been around as long as I, or longer. I will walk the Mill Pond Trail and the Nature Center often. I will cooperate more than compete. I will push the chairs back in place after writers' group at the library. I will write a poem or essay every week. I will rejoice in the company of those who share my values, while not shunning those who do not.

"I will count myself fortunate that I have survived the rigors of bringing up a family. I will allow myself to tear up a little when I think of the three women who happen to be my daughters. They are their own persons, dealing with their problems, reaching out to those around them, and often finding happiness as they make their way in the world.

"I will go to the July 5 evening concert at Veterans' Park Band Shell, eat ice cream, swat mosquitoes, stand and sing 'The Star Spangled Banner.' And listen as emcee Duane Germain reminds the children not to lose their parents on the way home."

I like going to Third Wednesday because I find a sense of achievement in reading my poems and essays and hearing others, and because others are getting to know me and welcome me, as I do them. And they don't have to know you to welcome you.

I think that's what "agrarian life and values" means. It has something to do with being part of the place where we live—and maybe even something to do with patriotism. It's why my attachment to this place, this arc of the globe, is so very deep.

viewpoint

ViewPoint VIEWpoint
ViewPOINT
Viewpoint

EASY TO HATE?

| Catholic postcards on the edge |

Donna Schaper (2009)

WILLIAM JAMES IN HIS MARVELOUS book, *The Varieties of Religious Experience*, speaks of the transition from Catholicism to Protestantism as the transition of the brocaded, artistic, colorful Baroque to one man in a black suit carrying a black book which he places on a plain table in an unornamented meeting house. His observations are on target. There is nothing perfect about Protestantism. Still it has a few values that might make a non-violent approach possible for those of us who spiritually and theologically value the right to choose an abortion. With Hillary Clinton, many of us think abortion should be safe, legal and rare. We also think it is a constitutionally guaranteed right. We also have respect for the constitutional promotion of a brocaded right to the separation of church and state.

When Roman Catholics take up a separate offering to remove abortion from federal funding and send their people home with an experience of the body of Christ – and a postcard to send to their congressional representatives – they violate both the body of Christ and the constitution. These are not small matters. Some of us are tempted to do more than growl: our stomachs churn at the deeper issue of one theology dominating another, illegally. Some of us find ourselves filling up with a kind of hate at injustice, abuse of the constitution, power gone amok. Some women are wearing T-shirts saying that we are feminists formerly for Obama. Not me: I see what he is up against. We surely understand the President's dilemma and praise our baroque friends for their protection of immigrants, gays, even women to a point in the new and overall positive health care bill. We sense ourselves eating different bread but not being part of a different body.

The reason hate is so tempting is that we are in fact so close to our Roman Catholic brothers and sisters. In the name of all that is good about Jesus and his international body, I spend a good bit of time praying for the hate and anger to subside. I also pray for the right lawsuit to stop my sisters and brothers from abusing the constitution by handing out post cards and taking up special offerings. Protestants may be plain but we frown on this sort of imperial moral legislating. We actually believe in the separation of Church and State and hope no (consenting and believing) Catholic will ever have an abortion.

It is not hateful to call to account. Nor is it hateful to enjoy the right to be different. While frowning on the temptation to hate a group of unmarried men, namely the bishops, who don't even represent their people, who believe more than not in the right to choose an abortion being protected by the federal government, we who are hurt and we who will be hurt by the lack of funding for abortions have a right to call for strong countervailing action. A good lawsuit against the postcards would go a long way towards resolving this dilemma. Then we might go back to living on a fair and even playing field when it comes to politics, theocracies and women's rights.

GOD'S HIT MEN

| When religion turns violent |

G. Jeffrey MacDonald (2002)

EVER SINCE KORAN-CARRYING HIJACKERS horrified the world a year ago by taking more than 3,000 lives in the name of God, people of faith have grappled to explain what seems inexplicable.

How could anyone kill himself and others in the name of a loving, merciful God?

The possibility seemed so foreign to the Western mind that it gave rise to a spate of articles about the great chasm of cultural differences separating East and West. Perhaps, it seemed, our cultures were doomed to clash over irreconcilable values.

One year after Sept. 11, however, we can see that faith-inspired violence wasn't born last year. This year's slaughter in the Middle East provides a haunting reminder that murder in the name of God dates to the days of Isaac and Ishmael, yet it has not ceased. Judging from the hundreds of lives lost in Hindu-Muslim clashes in India, it seems religious violence has an eerie capacity to transcend national boundaries as well as periods of history.

Americans may shudder more than most at religious violence because it seems so foreign to our shores, where one apartment building in Manhattan can peacefully accommodate adherents to every major faith. Yet killing in the name of God is hardly a new phenomenon here – a fact all too familiar to those who work at abortion clinics.

Since 1977, the nation's 4,500 abortion workers have reported 7 murders, 17 attempted murders, 41 bombings and 165 incidents of arson, according to the Religious Coalition for Reproductive Choice. Even though mainstream pro-life groups have roundly condemned such vigilantism, a handful of outspoken renegades continue to say those who kill the innocent unborn deserve to be killed themselves in righteous execution of God's justice.

In looking back to September 2001 and a little beyond, Americans might probe the mind of Christian abortion terrorists in order to shed light on the enigma that is those who kill innocents in Allah's name. In doing so, they might deem insanity rather than religious conviction to be the catalyst in most terrorism. But they might also discover how much those who practice religious violence have in common with those who obey a higher law than Caesar's – and with society at large.

To glimpse the mind of Americans willing to kill in God's name, visit www.armyofgod.com. Here, Pro-Life Virginia uses images of dripping blood, a photo of a bloody fetus and iconic flames of "eternal hell fire" awaiting abortionists to highlight scripture verses that seem to sanction vengeance against "babykillers."

"Do not I hate them, O Lord, that hate thee? And am I not grieved with those that rise up against thee? I hate them with a perfect hatred: I count them mine enemies" (Psalm 139:21-22). "Thou shalt die the deaths of the uncircumcised by the hand of strangers: for I have spoken it, saith the Lord GOD" (Ezekiel 28:10).

From here, visitors may click on the "Ode to Slepian," an account of the murder of "babykilling abortionist Barnett Slepian" in Amherst, New York in 1998.

"From the cold, the man watched babykiller Slepian inside his comfortable half-million dollar house... The man who watched: a godly, righteous man, could no longer sit passively by while this evil beast enjoyed the fruits of his depraved blood trade... He prayed, took aim, then calmly pulled the trigger. The sound of window glass shattering, a hollow thud, and a woman's scream coming from the house pierced the frigid air. He smiled. Hallelujah to the LORD. The mass murderer had been stopped!"

Is this rationale for murder akin to whatever compels group-sponsored suicide attacks on American and Israeli civilians? Or is the justification of murder in God's name a sign of individual pathology and nothing more? According to Professor Linda Heath, Director of Loyola University's Psychology of Crime and Justice program, the chief factor is more likely to be individual mental illness rather than a particular belief system.

"Those are such rare instances that we really can't generalize about why people do it," Heath said. "When one person breaks away and [commits murder], I don't feel comfortable saying that anything in that culture caused them to do that."

One possible example: John Salvi, the infamous shooter who killed two and injured five at a Brookline, Mass. abortion clinic in 1994. The 23-year-old's firm anti-abortion views may have stemmed from his Roman Catholic background, but psychiatrists and lawyers argued that his motivation grew out of his paranoid schizophrenia.

"The mental illness overrode everything," said J.W. Carney, Salvi's defense attorney. "What drove John Salvi was this belief that Catholics were being persecuted by a conspiracy made up of Free Masons and executives of British Petroleum [among others]... It would have been so much easier to explain if he were a religious zealot."

The prosecuting attorney in the case, John Kivlan, had called Salvi a "terrorist" as he successfully pursued a two-count murder conviction and a life sentence without parole, but he declined to comment for this story. Shortly after his sentencing, Salvi hung himself in prison.

Not every instance of religious violence, however, bears the fingerprints of a delusional soul. James Kopp "acted rationally in every way" before allegedly killing Slepian, according to Eerie County District

Attorney Frank J. Clark. In Clark's view, only one factor could have motivated this figure known in militant anti-abortion camps as "the atomic dog" – his fervent conviction that abortionists are evil murderers who must be stopped.

"Because of his zealous commitment to this movement, he felt this was something he was compelled to do," said Clark, whose staff is now collecting DNA evidence for Kopp's trial in 2003. "What would make somebody move from prayer to violence is something I'm not qualified to answer."

Kopp's cool rationality, coupled with a clean record except for non-violent, abortion-related incidents, suggests the unsettling possibility that a clear-headed person of deep faith may be capable of, or even disposed toward, murder in God's name. The same could be said for at least some of the 19 Sept. 11 hijackers, such as Mohammed Atta, whose profile bespeaks a meticulous planner.

If then mental illness is not always the precipitating factor in religious violence, believers must once again wonder whether harboring a passion for God's justice might sometimes set the stage for deadly deviance. Those who have observed criminal behavior for years say yes, while religious motives are relatively rare in U.S. crime, they can be among the deadliest worldwide.

"If we were to list motives that stir people to violence, religious motivation might be number one," Clark said. For examples, he cites Northern Ireland in the 20th century and the Crusades in the 11th century. Though this is his first religiously motivated case over 30 years as a prosecutor, he said, the prospect of more violence being done in God's name is always there.

"I tell my students, 'never underestimate the power of belief because human beings are capable of doing anything'," said Dr. Dale Lindekugel, Chairman of Eastern Washington University's Department of Sociology and Criminal Justice. "Certain kinds of belief can have a contagion effect," he said, producing "subcultures" that will endorse the use of violence under certain conditions.

Here it seems those who perpetrate religious violence may have quite a bit in common with the mainstream American believer. With the exception of die-hard pacifists who oppose the use of force in every case, practitioners of faith by and large accept a notion of "just war" as defined by Augustine of Hippo in the fifth century. Violence is justified, the theory holds, when all other options have been exhausted and other specific criteria are met. For the United States to bomb Afghanistan after 9/11 marked an example in which most of the nation's believers supported a violent response to an attack.

Believers are not only willing to condone violence as they did after 9/11, but they are also inclined to establish their own criteria – separate from the government's – when justifying their own use of violence. To kill when one's spouse or children are threatened, for instance, would represent a form of vigilante violence that most persons of faith would readily practice, according to Lindekugel. "I as a citizen hold a belief that deadly force is legitimated in pursuit of certain ideals."

So too do religious terrorists, Lindekugel said. "It's not a pathology at all. We might think their values [for which they'd kill] are pathological, but others think our values are pathological." Whether religious terrorists are targeting abortion clinics or grand symbols of American power, they embrace a common purpose: to use any means necessary to undo what they believe to be systemic evil.

The Army of God likens abortionists to Nazis, resolving to forcibly end today's holocaust of innocents. Fringe environmental groups push the envelope too, potentially in God's name, when they burn tree-harvesting facilities to the ground or spike trees in such a way that mill workers could be injured or killed as a result. In case after case, believers in a moral code above the one codified in state or federal law inevitably adhere to a hierarchy of values that might not mirror their neighbor's. And unless non-violence under all conditions happens to be a group's chief value, then resorting to violence to protect something else of value will forever endure as an apparently moral option.

Religious terrorism might be relatively rare in the United States because the nation's civil religion, or transcendent set of values for this diverse society, staunchly regards the killing of innocents as an unacceptable, evil act. In fact, governments at the state and federal levels are willing to put to death those who take the life of innocents. In the view of many a jury, such persons deserve to die. More than 1,000 detainees at Guantanamo Bay could face execution if convicted by a society that values some things more than human life.

Yet herein lies the most disturbing reality of a close examination of religious violence in its varied forms: to justify it to the satisfaction of the general populace, one merely has to show that the targeted "innocents" are in fact guilty of a heinous crime against God. American governments kill those guilty of murder. The Army of God supports killing those guilty of murdering the unborn. Al Qaeda kills those guilty of financing missiles and rifles for Israeli soldiers to use against Palestinians.

Each of us sees the other as guilty of violating that which we value above all else. Hence the violence we perpetrate against them is not terrorism because they are not in fact innocent. It is, in each perpetrator's mind, justice because they are guilty before God, whether or not Caesar's government has recognized that fact. And so it will be as long as so-called religious terrorists and so-called legitimate societies agree that violence can sometimes be justified.

ONE FAMILY'S VALUES

| 'Elite fundamentalists' embrace the amorality of power |

James Armstrong (2009)

A $1.1 MILLION, THREE-STOREY, ivy-covered, flag adorned, brick rowhouse stands at 133 C Street SE. It is within a stone's throw of the Library of Congress, congressional office buildings and the U.S. Capitol. It was once a convent. Today it is classified as a "church;" it is a tax-exempt rooming house for Congressmen and Senators who pay $600 a month for the privilege of living there and participating in its activities. It operates under the name of the Fellowship Foundation. Its residents and members are known as the Family. It came to the public's attention this summer when three notable public figures acknowledged extra-marital affairs and mentioned, in passing, the house on C Street.

First there was Sen. John Ensign of Nevada who confessed to a career-shattering affair. He had lived at the house and sought counsel there among his "brothers."

Then there was Gov. Mark Sanford of South Carolina who

disappeared from the face of the earth for several days. Neither his wife nor his staff knew where he was. It was rumored that he was tramping along the Appalachian Trail. Actually, he was in Buenos Aires with his Argentine mistress. When he returned, confronted by the media, he tearfully admitted the affair and mentioned the fact that earlier he had gone to the C Street house to look for answers.

NOT LONG THEREAFTER, Leisha Pickering filed for divorce, accusing her husband, Chip, a former Congressman from Mississippi, of "wrongful conduct" with a woman who had been his college sweetheart. He had lived at the C Street house, which became a trysting place for him and his extra-curricular girlfriend.

Each of these men, conservative Republicans, had stressed family values when running for public office. But the family values they talked about as politicians seemed far removed from the values of the Family on C Street they identified with.

The Family's values have been shaped and defined by two men, a Norwegian immigrant named Abraham (Abram) Vereide, and Douglas Coe, who became the Family/Fellowship leader when Vereide was "promoted to heaven" in 1969. The Family, its strange seventy-five year history, its stranger-still self-concept, and the tawdry behavior of some of its members, have come to our attention through a block-buster book, *The Family: the Secret Fundamentalism at the Heart of American Power,* by Jeff Sharlet, and by the reporting of MSNBC's Rachel Maddow. What exactly are the Family's values?

Secrecy, stealth and confidentiality. Insisting that secrecy is simply privacy, the Family is a self-described invisible network of fundamentalist followers of Christ in government, business and the military. Members see themselves as an organism rather than a formal organization. From the very beginning, in 1935, they determined to be "invisible;" to "submerge."

Those living at C Street are pledged to be loyal to one another. They will trust one another, rely upon one another, confess to one another, pray together, and vow that they will not talk about each other, or about the group and its activities, to anyone outside the brotherhood.

"The more invisible you are the more influence you will have."

Jesus only, or Jesus plus nothing. At first glance this may seem commendable, but it has nothing to do with the teachings of Jesus, the love-ethic, the parables of Jesus and his Sermon on the Mount. It is the Fact of Jesus, the Person of Christ, that is important. The Godhead is all wrapped up in Him as he reveals himself to "key persons," His chosen leaders. A friend said, "Doug (Coe) talks to Jesus man-to-man."

Do you remember how Gov. Sanford likened himself to King David during one of his press conferences? He came by that naturally. David Coe, Doug's son, speaking with a group of Family members, once said, "King David liked to do really, really bad things. Here's this guy who slept with another man's wife – Bathsheba, right? – and then basically murdered her husband...God *likes* the guy...If you're a person known to be around Jesus, you can go and do anything...We elect our leaders. Jesus elects us."

Key persons, powerful leaders, "the chosen." Believing that God's covenant with the Jews has been broken core members of the Family claim to be *the new chosen*. They call their belief system "elite fundamentalism" and insist that God has chosen certain powerful key men to direct the affairs of nations. Vereide was convinced he was called to go, not to the "down-and-out, but to the "up-and-out." Doug Coe said, "We work with power where we can, build new power where we can't." Sharlet writes, "Jesus plus nothing = power; invisible power, the long, slow, building power of a few brothers and sisters" (p. 256).

Power is amoral. Appealing to Romans 13, the Fellowship insists that all rulers are God-ordained. "Elite fundamentalists...did not care much about sin; they cared about salvation, a concept they understood in terms of nations, not souls, embodied by the rulers to whom God has given power, whether through ballots or bullets" (Sharlet, 220).

Both Abram Vereide and Doug Coe were fascinated by strong-arm dictators, and in some respects, sought to emulate them. Coe believed in the development of "cells," small group covenants. He said, "Look at Hitler, Lenin, Ho Chi Minh, bin Laden." They had forged covenants with their brothers. "Communists use cells as their basic structure. The Mafia operates like this." "Nazism started with seven guys around a table in the back of an old German Beer Hall. The world has been shaped so drastically by a few men...We need this same kind of stuff as Hitler and Lenin."

The Fellowship has cultivated prayer networks in Congress and sponsors cells around the world. Their supportive prayers surrounded men like Suharto in Indonesia, who murdered 500,000 of his countrymen; Pinochet in Chile (the Family's key man in Chile wrote after the murderous junta had overthrown duly elected President Salvador Allende, "The sun is just now beginning to shine again."); Papa Doc in Haiti; and the military dictator, General Park of South Korea. Coe worked closely with Frank Buchman of Moral Rearmament, who once said, "I thank God for a man like Hitler, who built a front line against the anti-Christ of communism."

Another Family value is **biblical capitalism.** The Family was founded in Seattle in 1935 by Vereide. He had been leading a prayer group of business men at the Pacific Union Club. He argued that "to the big man went strength, to the little man went need. Only the big man is capable of mending the world." He aligned himself with "the big man." He hated FDR's New Deal, seeing "Russian red running through it." He hated labor unions, personified on the West Coast by Dave Beck, the heavy-handed head of the Teamsters, and Harry Bridges, the Australian born, left-leaning, head of the IWW (the Wobblies), who championed the cause of longshoremen. The Family came into being to fight the New Deal and organized labor.

"Biblical capitalism" weds scripture and currency. Its blind acceptance of unregulated capitalism, and its courtship of captains of industry like Henry Ford, more than matches Ayn Rand's extreme devotion to unbridled capitalism (although she would have flippantly rejected the "biblical" reference).

And, **world conquest.** Dan Coe, Doug's son, speaking to a group of Family members at Ivanwald, a house not unlike that on C Street, said, "You guys are here to learn how to rule the world." Congressional members of the Family, as well as its core leaders, have flown around the world, sometimes at the expense of the Family, blurring the dividing wall between church and state, planting and nurturing prayer cells.

Sharlet writes, "The family's long-term project of worldwide government under God is more ambitious than Al Qaeda's dream of a Sunni empire...not a walled off community, but an empire; not one to come but one that already stretches around the globe, the soft empire of American dollars, and more subtly, American gods." It is Manifest Destiny writ large.

THE NATIONAL PRAYER BREAKFAST was inaugurated in 1953, following Dwight Eisenhower's election to the Presidency. It continues to be one of the few visible "ministries" of the Family. Abram Vereide joined a handful of others, in starting the tradition. Every February some 3000 notable, representing scores of nations and corporate interests, pay $425. each to attend. Today Doug Coe, always far removed from the spotlight, "puts the whole thing together,"

Grace Nelson, a member of the Foundation Board, was once the organizer of the Florida Governor's Prayer Breakfast. She was also a member of the same Family prayer cell that Hillary Clinton participated in when she was in the Senate. Clinton is one of a handful of Democrats who is or was related to the Family. Sen. Bill Nelson, Grace's husband, is another one. I wrote him recently, identifying myself as a fellow Christian, a former President of the Florida Council of Churches and a lifelong Democrat. I wrote, "I would deeply appreciate a word from you about how you view the Family and how you and your wife Grace became involved in its life and outreach." I have had no response. He remains "submerged."

UMC NEEDS A "THIRD WAY" TO HEAL ITSELF

Cynthia B. Astle (2003)

A CONTROVERSIAL NEW BOOK released in May, *United Methodism@Risk*, contends that The United Methodist Church is in danger of a conservative takeover similar to that which has captured the Southern Baptist Convention.

As a professional observer of the denomination for more than 15 years, I concur heartily that the denomination is at risk—but not in the way that the backers of *United Methodism@Risk* assert.

The real issue before United Methodists, as evidenced by the actions and publications of the denomination's right and left wings, is how much longer the mass of United Methodists will permit extremists to frame the church's life and work. In this situation, the leaders of both wings have sinned grievously, first against one another and then against the church at large, by word and deed.

United Methodists should not be deceived by smokescreens of "doctrine" or "homosexuality" or "abortion" or any other topic. What's really at issue is power—power to say what the church believes and power to enforce adherence to what those in power say the church believes.

Since this column appeared originally in *The United Methodist Reporter*, leaders of both conservative and liberal groups in the church have contacted me to deny the validity of this thesis. I found it fascinating that in attempting to refute my thesis, both representatives insisted that having power isn't necessarily a bad thing, that the intention of the respective groups is to use power to influence the direction of the church. Call me thick-headed, but to me this common rebuttal sounds lot like my thesis – what's at issue, fundamentally, is gaining and using power in the church to assure that one's own perspective triumphs.

In this, the conservative wing has been the best organized, the most vocal and the most active. It also has employed one of the most shameful tactics, bringing church trials against pastors and bishops who dispute, by word or action, current United Methodist stances.

Some conservative leaders have contended that the church's judicial system offers the only means of assuring doctrinal accountability in the United Methodist system. Yet using the church's judicial system to press for doctrinal purity has cost The United Methodist Church thousands of dollars for legal expenses that could better have been spent for evangelism and mission.

Nor can the church's liberal wing claim moral high ground. Anyone who rationally questions the wisdom of some of the liberal agenda—and the left has an agenda as does the right—is automatically demeaned as a "conservative" or "homophobic" or "right-winger" or worse. Daring to exhibit intellectual independence from left-wing jingoism has led to besmirching honest Christians of integrity.

Those who've defied the church's stances have caused grievous wounds across the denomination—and played right into the conservatives' hands, further exacerbating the conflict. The left may be less organized than the right, but its tactics are no less damaging to the church's soul.

Clinging to life in the middle are those of us who chose not to identify with any of the groups forming the right and left wings of the church. We fear doctrinal tyranny as much as we fear dictatorial tolerance without moral judgment.

In fact, "fear" may be the operative word in this conflict. The left fears the right; the right fears the left. The centrists fear both extremes because, as an African proverb rightly says, "When elephants fight, the grass suffers."

Indeed The United Methodist Church has suffered horribly through the past 30-odd years of this constant war. There's a lot of "dysfunctional family" dynamic in United Methodists' political behavior, like spoiled "children" breaking the rules and causing "parents" to exert authority. Like a mother in such a family dynamic, I'm proposing the church call "time out," because this constant conflict has rendered the denomination incapable of fulfilling its mission: To make disciples of Jesus Christ who proclaim God's love for all humanity and who demonstrate God's love individually and in society.

I find my argument about the damage done to the church bolstered by some sobering numbers released in May by the General Council on Finance and Administration in a report, "Making Disciples for Jesus Christ: A Statistical Review of the State of the Church." Consider:

- ✓ Nearly 41 percent of United Methodist congregations in the United States didn't receive ONE new member by profession of faith or restoration from inactive status in 2000. Yet local congregations today are keeping to themselves some 83 cents of every dollar contributed, with the remaining 17 cents going to support ministries beyond the local church. Conservatives contend that keeping the money "at home" is one way to protest the liberalism of the denomination's leadership. Yet how is this money being spent locally, since it doesn't appear to fulfill the church's mission to make disciples for Christ, which is the announced goal of evangelicals?
- ✓ In 1980, there were 43 United Methodists per 1,000 Americans. Today there are 29 United Methodists per 1,000 Americans—a 33 percent decline. This figure is more

shocking when we consider that there are United Methodist congregations in 3,003 of the 3,171 counties in the United States—more than any other denomination. Why doesn't anyone want to join us if we're so available to them? There are many reasons, but I'm convinced that one of them is our constant bickering with one another.

After years of battle, there remains hope of a "third way," if we have the courage to take it. It is the way of self-denial taught and modeled by Jesus.

Even the most cursory study of the Gospel of Matthew, for instance, calls up a dynamic of self-denial that seeks to restore relationships:

"You have heard that it was said to those of ancient times, 'You shall not murder' and 'whoever murders shall be liable to judgment.' But I say to you that if you are angry with a brother or sister, you will be liable to the council; and if you say, 'You fool,' you will be liable to the hell of fire. So when you are offering your gift at the altar, if you remember that your brother or sister has something against you, leave your gift there before the altar and go; first be reconciled to your brother or sister, and then come and offer your gift." (Mt. 5: 21-24)

" . . . You have heard that it was said, 'You shall love your neighbor and hate your enemy.' But I say to you, Love your enemies and pray for those who persecute you, so that you may be children of your Father in heaven . . . For if you love only those who love you, what reward do you have? Do not even the tax collectors do the same? And if you greet only your brothers and sisters, what more are you doing than others? Do not even the Gentiles do the same?" (Mt. 5:43-47)

Of course these extracts show how all of us selectively quote Scripture to bolster our own arguments. In this instance, however, these texts show the "third way" that Jesus taught and lived.

The sad truth about this ongoing struggle for power is that many are giving up on the church because it seems only to fight all the time, instead of using the Christian conflict resolution strategies outlined above. Many United Methodists lament the so-called "disconnect" between denominational leaders and people in the pews, but I contend the greater "disconnect" is between Christian ideals and those who are supposed to be practicing them.

This dissonance between preaching and practice is most clearly seen in the church's Machiavellian politics. The self-righteous "ends justifying the means" behavior of United Methodist factions has to stop.

Taking a "third way" would mean that each extreme lays down its weapons of half-truths and outright lies about each other and the church at large. It means we would give up our own agendas, left, right or center.

It means we would remember that the church does not belong to us humans, but to God alone. It means we would repent of our internecine battles that have barred God's boundless love, manifest in the Risen Christ, from being made known in the world through us.

Following Jesus' way means that we would empty ourselves of our own will, as Jesus did in Gethsemane, to be obedient to God's will. Determining *together* what God's will is for the church means that we would abandon our General Conference legislative processes in favor of a time of prayerful discernment.

The General Commission on the General Conference has proposed an operating plan somewhat like this, but the commission's proposal doesn't go far enough.

Instead, The United Methodist Church may benefit mightily if the 2004 General Conference doesn't adopt *any* legislation, except a budget, when it meets next year in Pittsburgh. All that's needed would be a motion to table the legislative agenda—again excepting necessary financial matters—to the 2008 meeting.

Then General Conference delegates could devote themselves to prayer, worship and genuine "holy conferencing" about God's will for the future of the people called United Methodist. Thus they would engender the spiritual healing of the denomination, breaking our self-destructive cycle of political abuse and character assassination.

The prospect of abandoning traditional legislation and Roberts' Rules of Order for a discernment process seriously threatens many. We don't know how to do this; we don't know how to talk with one another about what we think we're hearing when seeking God's guidance through prayer. We don't trust each other to be truthful in discernment. We're afraid of what kind of answers we'll get.

All these uncertainties are the point of the exercise. We need to humble ourselves before God, and that involves surrendering to the awe-filled experience of the Divine. We need to humble ourselves before one another and make room for God's sovereignty over the church—not our schemes, not our plans, not our agendas, not our politics.

We're past due for a churchwide act of repentance and contrition for our political sins. Are we courageous enough to take such a radical step of faith?

THE KNIFE

| Accountability both hurts and heals |

Robert Shetterly (2007)

> *"Thank God our time is now when wrong*
> *Comes up to face us everywhere.*
> *Never to leave us till we take*
> *The longest stride of soul we ever took."*
>
> – Christopher Fry

THE GREATEST THREAT NOW, it seems to me, both to our democratic republic and our spiritual wellbeing, is the cowardly refusal of people in power to seek accountability for their acts. I purposely said "seek accountability."

Common people must necessarily have the courage to hold the powerful accountable. But a principled person seeks a reckoning, desires an honest tabulation for the virtue of his or her acts, knowing that history will eventually separate the honest from the knavish as surely as blood from snake oil.

I thought it might be instructive to consider this subject through one of the great American prophetic paintings of the 19th century, Thomas Eakins' *The Gross Clinic*. Painted in 1875 when Eakins was 35, it celebrates the Philadelphia surgeon, Dr. Samuel David Gross, from whom Eakins had learned anatomy.

Many people found the monumental painting disturbing, even repulsive, when it was first exhibited. Many people do today. The dramatic setting is a darkened surgical amphitheater. Lighted from above, it conveys a sense of spiritual significance reminiscent of Rembrandt's paintings of Christ in the Temple.

An operation is being performed on the left leg of a young man who is lying on the operating table. His naked legs and thin buttocks are exposed to the viewer. His body appears as quiescent and vulnerable as a lamb on an Old Testament altar. The painting has the ominous portent of the moment when God interceded to save Isaac from Abraham's sacrificial knife.

But here, ironically, Dr. Gross makes the cut because his knife is intended to prolong life rather than end it. The faith being celebrated is in scientific exploration, the skill and wisdom of the surgeon, and the desire to expand the limits of what's possible to help another person.

Dr. Gross, standing and heroically dominating the scene like George Washington crossing the Delaware, has just made a deep incision down to the bone of the boy's lower left thigh and has turned away from the procedure to address the audience of medical students seated in the dark, pew-like rows above him. He holds a short scalpel in his right hand. Both the scalpel and his fingers up to the second joint glisten with the boy's fresh red blood. The doctor's willingness to wear the boy's blood, to go to the bone, suggests a profound ritual of the search for truth.

Just below Dr. Gross's right elbow sits the diminutive figure of a woman dressed in black — the boy's mother. She buries her face in her left arm out of fear and squeamishness. If there is another sound in this somber painting besides the doctor's calm explanation, it is the mother's muffled whimpering. No one consoles her; the focus is on healing the sick, not the fearful. She is present to witness and support her son, but can do neither. Eakins meant her to signify the reaction of affection and sentiment without knowledge—a kind of caring that winces and looks away when most needed. In fact, the contrast between her hidden face and Dr. Gross's powerful presence—think of Frederick Douglass or John Brown, Sojourner Truth, Martin Luther King, Jr., or William Sloane Coffin—emphasizes the quality of character necessary to confront and deal with diseased reality and is a source of the painting's intense energy.

Dr. Gross is middle aged. His head is haloed by his graying hair, which stands out as though electrified by his generative thoughts. Light from a skylight far overhead illuminates his high, radiant forehead, the bridge of his nose and his bloody hand. His demeanor is one of confidence, authority, courage, mission, and integrity. Obviously, Eakins wanted to impress the viewer with the doctor's skill, the intensity of his dedication to both heal and teach.

I suspect also that Eakins identified with the doctor, implying that the doctor's red-fingered grasp of the scalpel is not unlike his own on the brush—that in both professions one must be courageous enough to dip one's hands in blood, either literally or figuratively. More important, though, is the sought after burden of responsibility. The surgeon diagnoses, cuts and attempts to heal in public.

This is a transparency that means just that, and not the slippery shell- game transparency promoted today that really means secrecy, hypocrisy and sanctimonious irresponsibility. Imagine for a moment the face of George W. Bush or Dick Cheney or Pat Robertson collaged in to replace the face of Dr. Gross.

No more needs to be said. Imagine your own.

EAKINS HAS EMPHASIZED THE BLOOD on the doctor's hand to ritualize the painting, to stress the sacred metaphor of the cost that must be paid in the search for truth and well-being. The patient/citizen offers his body and faith; the doctor/priest/ politician takes on the burden of healing and protecting blood and life.

For me, today, the political metaphor is more important than the medical or religious. Like the boy on the operating table, our body politic is infected to its very bones. Our plagued and weakened democratic skeleton barely supports the flaccid, overweight flesh of our arrogant, preposterously compromised myth. People with political prominence are either reveling in the corruption or denying its seriousness by offering superficial cures. They are the classic co-dependent enablers. The pathetic media treats them with respect and deference while it scoffs at or ignores those voices that diagnose the sickness and prescribe the necessary radical treatments.

Martin Luther King, Jr., once described non-violence as "the sword that heals" and he said that it's a sword that "ennobles the man who wields it." The same could be said of truth and accountability—they are the alloy that must be forged into the sword that heals. When people of power don't demand truth and accountability for themselves and their peers, they demonstrate that they have no respect for the system they pretend to venerate. They forfeit any respect that might be accorded them. The longer the people leave them in power, the more damage is done to the integrity of the system. And the longer the people leave them in power, the more we demonstrate that we have no respect for that system.

There is much to be learned from the good Doctor Gross. William Sloane Coffin used to say that true compassion demands action. Otherwise it is merely sentimental. A person who identifies the sickness of a situation, agonizes over it and does nothing, might as well be the boy's mother in Eakins' painting—so absorbed in squeamish grief as to be unable to be of any help. Now, as Christopher Fry says, that "... wrong comes up to face us everywhere/ ...we must take/ The longest stride of soul we ever took." The first stride is the insistence on accountability, political and moral.

AT WAR WITH PLEASURE

| Embrace our bodies to lay down our arms |

Beverly Dale (2011)

MANY ANY PEOPLE ASSUME that the best way to protect a nation is to have a strong defense and the latest military technology regardless of the cost. Some people think killing the enemy or conquering a nation with dangerous leadership is a necessary solution either to end conflict or to bring peace.

In fact, the United States of America has so frequently engaged in warmongering that as citizens, we have become comfortable with two concurrent wars in Afghanistan and Iraq, playing war games of intimidation off the coast of Korea, leading forces against Libya and hosting 856 military bases over the planet.[1]

As a feminist clergy I have studied violence in the context of sexuality and our views of our bodies, but especially women's bodies and sexuality in Christianity. After decades of research, I am convinced that our society's warped view of bodily pleasure, supported by the repressive teachings of the Church, have turned us into the bloody warmongering state we have become.

For example, what about our cultural passivity toward violence as entertainment, whether it occurs in the video games for children or on big movie screens? We allow explicit and bloody violence for children's consumption in media, but we censor nude bodies and sexual contact. What keeps us from defining violence as pornography?

We seldom consider the price we pay with our own humanity when we embrace violence and yield to warmongering tactics to bully friends and foes alike As one veteran wrote, "The experience of killing your fellow human beings—whether innocent civilians or enemy combatants—fundamentally changes how you see yourself. War makes you doubt your own goodness; life itself seems cheap and meaningless."[2] When we fail to consider what violence does to us as individuals and as a society we have clearly dismissed the warnings about the military industrial complex from former President Dwight Eisenhower, himself a general during World War II.[3]

Although many in the Church say the violence of war is unavoidable, it is instructive to heed the advice of the last remaining WWI veteran Harry Patch, who said of his war experience, "At the end, the peace was settled round a table, so why the hell couldn't they do that at the start without losing millions of men?"[4] And the war-weary statesman, Winston Churchill, during WWII said, "It is better to talk, talk, talk than to war, war, war."

But despite such warnings, the Church in the United States exists in a militarized country that embraces spending $135 billion on weapons programs[5] even as those in power seek to cut pensions for the aged, welfare for the poor, and benefits to immigrants, documented or not. Declaring ourselves to be the world's policeman, this nation consumed 45 percent of the entire world's military spending between 2004 and 2007. Why do we as a society embrace violence and engage in war when we have been repeatedly warned against it, and when it is clearly not rational?

THE ANSWER MAY LIE IN OUR EVOLUTIONARY HERITAGE. Though researchers cannot be sure when we changed our minds, anthropologists think that *H. sapiens* has not always chosen war to settle conflicts. Christopher Ryan, Ph.D., and Cacilda Jethá, M.D., are evolutionary psychologists who recently published the New York Times best seller *Sex at Dawn: The Prehistoric Origins of Modern Sexuality* (New York, Harper, 2010). Ryan and Jethá propose that the shift to embrace violence appears to be related to our movement from being a forager species to an agrarian one.[6] Apparently the human species went from peace-loving to violence-prone, from being sexually free and egalitarian to sexually repressive and hierarchical, from female- empowered leadership to male-led domineering societies when we claimed land for individuals instead of sharing it in communities. Even today, in the few remaining forager societies with sufficient resources, people tend to work only half a day and spend the remainder of time in social and pleasurable activities in peaceful, small egalitarian communities.

In addition, two primate species, bonobos and chimps (when freely studied in the forest, not studied where humans disrupt their food sharing patterns), both live as sexually free and female-led in small, peaceful communities using sexual pleasure and cooperation as incentives. These primates share 97 percent of our DNA.

Thus it appears from separate studies of current forager societies and of our primate cousins that the biblical vision of a Garden of Eden still exists. In other words, somewhere along our developmental path, human beings chose war and violence instead of shared pleasure.

According to the research of Dr. James W. Prescott, the choice for violence and warmongering is directly related to societal aversion to pleasure and the level of abhorrence of uninhibited sexual expression.[7] Prescott's study of the world's societies' views toward sexuality and their correlated level of violence shows that violence is intimately related to sexual repression. He suggests that violence may stem from deprivation of somatosensory pleasure either in infancy or in adolescence, but that the adolescent experience of repression outweighs and obviates the infant's pleasurable experience. Prescott writes, "Physically affectionate human societies are highly unlikely to be physically violent." In fact, there's a 25,000-to-1 probability that violence declines in societies that value physical affection to infants and tolerance of premarital sex.

The links between feminine sexuality, female leadership, and non-violence are further supported by the work of archeological anthropologist Maria Gimbutas in *The Language of the Goddess* (New York, Thames & Hudson 2001)[8] and by historian Riane Eisler in *The Chalice and the Blade* (San Francisco, HarperOne, 1988).[9] Their research and that from a variety of other disciplines challenges our notions of the inevitability of violence. These studies also propose an intertwining connection of increased violence with repressed or denied sexuality and pleasure.

This deep-seated yet thwarted biological drive for physical pleasure explains in part why the Sept. 11, 2001 terrorists were given the prospect of an afterlife with access to multiple female virgins for sexual relations. It may also explain why at least one of them went to a strip club the night before his suicidal deed; his impending act of martyrdom entitled him to enjoy women as sex objects.

The research underscores the tendency for male soldiers in times of war to be tempted to rape as they pillage and why rape is now a preferred weapon of intimidation in the war-torn Democratic Republic of the Congo. It explains why a female U.S. soldier stands a greater chance of being sexually assaulted by her own colleagues than by enemies or civilians. According to the Pentagon, there was a 9 percent increase in sexual assaults among the military in 2008, but a 25 percent increase for those military women serving in Iraq and Afghanistan.[10] The columnist Chalmers Johnson writes, "The U.S Military has created a worldwide sexual playground for its personnel and protected them to a large extent from the consequences of their behavior."[11]

However, Military Sexual Trauma (MST) is nothing new for the citizenry. As Johnson notes, low-income Japanese woman living near the U.S. military base in Okinawa have endured an average of 350 sexual aggressions annually by U.S. soldiers throughout the 64 years of the base's existence.

This intimate interconnection between violence and sexuality is born out in the microcosm of the family that experiences child abuse.

Research has shown that those who abuse their children are themselves sensually or sexually pleasure- deprived. The idea is that without pleasure and sexual expression of some form in our lives we will turn aggressive.[12] At a more mundane level we already know we link sex and aggression by accepting and perpetuating the idea that members of athletic sport teams should forgo sex before games.[13] So the research seems clear: sexual repression easily leads to an embrace of violence, whereas a society with a focus on sexual plentitude with fewer restrictions on pleasure is less violent. In other words, it appears that the slogan "Make love, not war" of the sexual revolution was absolutely on target.

In fact, laboratory research shows that with animals the presence of pleasure actually inhibits the violence centers of the brain. According to Prescott, when the brain's pleasure circuits are "on" then the violence circuits are "off," and vice versa. Among animals, he writes, "a pleasure-prone personality rarely displays violence or aggressive behaviors, and a violent personality has little ability to tolerate, experience, or enjoy sensuously pleasing activities."[14]

This scientific research poses a major challenge for religion being used to justify sexual repression. If a religion views pleasure as the suspected first step on a downhill slide into sinful hedonism, it can easily justify sexual repression and be more likely to condone violence. This may well explain why evangelical American believers are most adamant about preventing sexual activity among young adults by trying to limit access to contraception and science-based sex information at the same time they favor the death penalty and to support war. Pastors who condemn sexual expression in their sermons should not be surprised to find their parishioners also support violent public policies.[15]

Research also makes it clear that warmongering itself is a sign of the perversion of passion into violence. It is important to remember that when this happens "the claustrophobic fusions of abuse and oppression can be mistaken for love and intimacy," according to Christian theologian Rita Nakashima Brock.[16] She notes that "violence forms an intense emotional bond" and this can seriously damage or destroy capacities for healthy intimacy. As the *New York Times* documented,

Iraqi war veterans returning with PTSD, diagnosed or not, continued their violent behavior and chose perhaps for a variety of reasons to murder those closest to them: parents, wives, children and fellow soldiers.[17]

Brock reminds us that just as membranes hold together the body, social "membranes" hold a community together. These membranes can become ruptured and toxic to others. From a faith perspective, she writes that, "violence damages the human soul—the complex thinking, feeling, inspirited, embodied self each of us struggles to integrate, to make whole." Rather than glorifying warmongering or soldiers trapped in a toxic culture of violence, we would do well as people of faith to remember that a leaning toward violence emerges from instincts that "arise from violated membranes, from broken selves," Brock writes. From a Christian perspective, this is clearly not the world of mutual love and justice that Jesus taught and that God intends.

If we want a less violent world we have to commit to embracing sexual and sensual pleasures as being as important as eating and drinking. We must focus on building an egalitarian society and dismantle the status hierarchies and income inequalities preventing us from the vision of a compassionate community where all have enough to fill their needs.

Proverbs 29:18 teaches, "Without a vision, the people perish." The vision can get sullied since all major faith traditions have holy writ that can be used to justify violence and control of women or other "sexual deviants."[18] However, each faith tradition also has sacred teachings that affirm peacemaking, harmonious egalitarian relationships, and appreciation for the gifts of pleasure and responsible sexuality. People of faith share a vision of one humanity living in many peace-filled communities.

Taking the research on primates or on forager societies as insightful clues and our sacred peacemaking traditions as our mandate, we must be willing to share resources with one another to create small communities of abundance and embrace pleasure, forsaking all efforts toward sexual repression. We must recognize the interrelationships of these social membranes that hold us together. In doing so, like the bonobos and our ancestors, we will begin to value pleasure over conflict, egalitarian sharing over competition, and peacemaking over warmongering. We will be about the business of turning swords into plowshares as envisioned by the prophet Isaiah. It is a choice we can and must make. Anything less will be the genocide of our species.

REFERENCES

1. Danes, Anita, "The Cost of the Global U.S. Military Presence," published July 3, 2009 by FPIF, a project of the Institute for Policy Studies.
2. Meehan, Shannon, "Distant Wars, Constant Ghosts," New York Times, March 5, 2010.
3. Eisenhower, Dwight D., Military Industrial Complex speech 1961 http://www.h-net.org/~hst306/documents/indust.html.
4. "The Last of the Noblest Generation," The Independent UK, July 26, 2010 http://www.independent.co.uk/news/uk/home-news/the-last-of-the-noblest-generation-1761467.html.
5. "What Would You Do With an Extra $70 billion?" NY Times, April 3, 2011.
6. Ryan, Christopher and Cacilda Jethá, *Sex at Dawn: The Prehistoric Origins of Modern Sexuality* (New York, Harper Collins, 2010).
7. Prescott, James W., "Body Pleasure and the Origins of Violence," Bulletin of the Atomic Scientists, November 1975, p 10-20. http://www.violence.de/prescott/bulletin/article.html
8. Gimbutas, Marija and Joseph Campbell, *The Language of the Goddess* (New York, Thames & Hudson, 2001).
9. Eisler, Riane, *The Chalice and the Blade* (San Francisco, HarperOne, 1988).
10. Herbert, Bob, "The Great Shame," New York Times, March 20, 2009.
11. Johnson, Chalmers, "Three Good Reasons to Liquidate Our Empire and Ten Steps to Take to Do So," www.tomdispatch.com, July 30, 2009.
12. Prescott, James, "Child Abuse: Slaughter of the Innocents," Hustler, October 1977.
13. Lovgren, Stefan, "Sex and Sports: Should Athletes Abstain Before Big Events?" National Geographic News, Feb. 22, 2006.
14. Ibid. Prescott, 1975.
15. Zylstra, Sarah Eekhoff "Capital Doubts," Christianity Today, Feb. 19, 2008.
16. Brock, Rita Nakashima, "Whither Ecumenism? A Theology for Ecumenism Beyond Violence," Mid-Stream, The Ecumenical Movement Today, Volume 41, Number 1, January 2002.

17. Sontag, Deborah and Lizette Alvarez, "War Torn," NY Times, Jan. 13, 2008.
18. Ternan, Oliver, *Violence in the Name of God, Religion in an Age of Conflict* (Maryknoll, NY, Orbis Books, 2003).

PURVEYORS OF FALSE MEMORY

| The IRD versus the church |

Thom White Wolf Fassett (2002)

ON NOVEMBER 18, 1995 AT 10:29 A.M., I stood in the White House Oval Office with my hand on the back of the President of the United States as one of a small group of religious leaders encircling him in prayer. Within the week, a Washington-based group called the Institute on Religion and Democracy (IRD) attacked us for praying with the president.

Since its inception in the earlier 1980s, the IRD has attacked mainline denominations as they sought to fulfill the mandates of their respective governing bodies—all the while proclaiming, that "religious freedom is the cornerstone of human rights and democracy." Hence, this particular Nov. 18 attack on religious freedom was a surprising new strategy. It left us more deeply convinced that political, not religious, motives drove the staff and supporters of IRD. The real offense eliciting the attack that day was the fact that religious leaders were asking the president to veto a welfare bill that would remove the social safety net for untold numbers of women and children. This was not politically acceptable to the IRD.

Having spent nearly 20 years in Washington, D.C., as a staff person with the social action agency of The United Methodist Church, I was no stranger to the goals and activities of the IRD. As the agency's chief executive for more than 12 years, I became intimately acquainted with the organization as its leaders routinely launched assaults on me personally and on The United Methodist Church. Nothing but a complete takeover of the church seemed to be their objective.

We now know that the IRD's takeover agenda includes not only The United Methodist Church but the Episcopal Church and the Presbyterian Church (USA) as well. This is made clear, in a recent privately circulated 14-page IRD document titled, "Reforming America's Churches Project, 2001-2004."

In the document, which is written as a funding proposal, IRD officials claim that liberal theology has failed the mainline churches, resulting in the loss of millions of members. During 2001- 2004, they claim there will be "rare opportunity to redirect these churches away from their reflexive alliance with the political left and back towards classical Christianity." The paper is replete with discussions of "the right" and "the left" and political language that polarizes people across the spectrum of religious conviction.

Declaring that they will spend more than $3.6 million over the next four years to promote their agenda, they anticipate contributions from United Methodists of at least $500,000.

This is nothing new. During its 20 years of existence, the IRD has not changed its goals. Founded in 1981 by political activists and evangelical religious leaders, the organization was formed to investigate and oppose certain social action programs of the mainline Protestant churches and became absorbed in tracking the social action funds managed by the denominations. The founding document of the IRD was a report on the funding of outside groups by The United Methodist Church written by David Jessup, at that time a new member of The United Methodist Church living in Silver Spring Maryland.

Jessup's report, "Preliminary Inquiry Regarding the Financial

Contributions to Outside Political Groups by Boards and Agencies of The United Methodist Church (UMC), 1977-1979," became the basis of debate and ongoing inquiry within the church concerning its social action expenditures. Although, according to available records, the document was shared with a few delegates attending the General Conference of 1980, no legislative action was taken at that time. Significantly, the Good News Forum, an evangelical caucus within the UMC, supported the Jessup document because it reflected their ongoing concerns over a number of years.

In those early days, the board membership of IRD was dominated by well-known intellectuals such as sociologist Peter Berger and authors Richard John Neuhaus and Michael Novak. The board membership was variously associated with the Coalition for a Democratic Majority, the American Enterprise Institute, Social Democrats, U.S.A., and other groups interested in combating communism.

These high-profile board members eventually abandoned the IRD, ostensibly because it turned out not to be the vehicle they had anticipated for their political ambitions. Others remained for a time: David Jessup, Paul Morell, Virginia Law Shell, Ira Gallaway and, notably, Ed Robb of the Robb Evangelistic Association, who galvanized the relationship between Good News and IRD and now, by implication, other UMC church-related "renewal" movements. This would include "Renew," the women's organization now attacking United Methodist Women across the nation.

Ed Robb's son, James, staffed the IRD offices for a period of time. It is important to note that Good News Magazine has, from the beginning of IRD, carried sympathetic articles and harsh critiques of the official structures of the UMC, much in keeping with the political objectives of IRD. At that time in the IRD's early days, two graduate students hired by United Methodist and United Church of Christ agencies concluded in their research that the IRD's board was composed of two groups, the Social Democrats/USA and its associates, and the leaders of Good News.

IRD funding patterns continue today as they have from the beginning with contributions from individuals, evangelical groups and foundations such as the Smith Richardson Foundation and the

Pittsburgh-based foundation of Richard Mellon Scaife. Whatever success the IRD achieves in implementing its programs today is based primarily on the co-option of faith-based organizations to realize its political goals.

Its leaders serve, rather like "recovered memory" therapists who tell United Methodists that their church has taken ridiculous and abhorrent positions on the most critical issues facing humankind today. Hearing this, members who typically do not have their church's teachings in front of them to refute the allegations, react strongly and negatively only to learn afterwards that they are victims of "false memory syndrome." That is, they have been the pawns in a very unethical game of dissembling, obfuscation and outright lies by a secular political organization that more closely resembles a religious caucus of the right wing of the Republican Party.

I belong to no political party. Rather, I write as a United Methodist Christian and out of a context of extensive experience in the church. In previous years and during my term as chief executive of the General Board of Church and Society (now a target for elimination by IRD), I had invited IRD officials to participate with religious leaders and denominational coalitions in Washington to work together toward common goals; these related to various advocacies and national legislation projects designed to implement the Social Principles of The United Methodist Church and the mandates of the General Conference. However, they have refused to share in any work of the UMC but continue to conduct pamphleteering and media strategies opposing most moral and ethical imperatives articulated by the church's governing body. Likewise, over the years, I extended invitations to the Good News Forum to dialogue with the General Board of Church and Society around critical issues of mutual concern facing the church. Good News never responded to the invitations.

Embedded in the IRD is the United Methodist Action Committee, which church members often mistake as an official organization of The United Methodist Church. Along with the IRD itself, it is a privately funded, self-appointed, secular lobbying group that attacks the Bible-based, prophetic efforts authorized by the General Conference. They stand in sharp contrast to the church's social action agency; the General Board of Church and Society, for example, has over 60 elected members from the denomination who are engaged in ministries officially mandated and paid for by the church (see particularly paragraphs 1002 and 1004 of *The 2000 Book of Discipline*). These directives are firmly planted in the historic constitution and the doctrinal statements of the church.

The IRD has cultivated powerful media spokespersons to extend its agenda. Brit Hume of Fox Television and syndicated columnist Cal Thomas are but two examples of media celebrities who frequently and uncritically pass on to the American public political analysis produced by the IRD without checking their sources or the veracity of their findings. These relationships have ill served both the UMC constituency and the secular public by promoting IRD's questionable political views as though they were verifiable researched issues related to mainline (United Methodist) religious organizations.

For instance, the General Board of Church and Society shipped nearly 500 donated computers to Cuba for Christian brothers and sisters to form a healthcare network; the purpose was to track aspirin, antibiotics, and other medicines to help save the lives of people. This shipment was achieved through tedious negotiations with the United States and the legal transport of these computers to Cuba with the assistance of the government of the United States. The IRD charged us, however, with shipping these computers to "communist Cuba, despite the US embargo."

The IRD mantra appropriately includes attacks on totalitarian states and the lack of the free exercise of religion. But its officials took no notice upon my return from Cuba, having negotiated for seven hours personally with Fidel Castro around principles of religious practice in Cuba. Little notice is given to the fact that Methodist and Presbyterian churches are the fastest growing churches in Cuba, in some part the result of our ecumenical lobbying of the Castro government to loosen restraints on religious practice.

Issues of homosexuality and abortion rights have been the bread-and-butter issues for both the IRD and Good News. These two issues have netted them more financial contributions and more members than all of the other issues combined. This has been achieved only by obfuscation and publication of disinformation to the church's constituents.

The policies of The United Methodist Church on these issues, however, are clear and straightforward. Anyone actually reading them could not possibly misinterpret them. So rampant are the misinterpretations of these issues by IRD, however, and so effective are they in broadly communicating their misinterpretation that they have opened a rift in the family of faith that will not soon be healed.

CONFRONTING OUR FEARS

| A conservative laments the erosion of dialogue |

Stephen W. Rankin (2004)

A FEW MONTHS AGO on a Saturday morning, as my wife and I enjoyed a leisurely coffee conversation with a houseguest, I received an unexpected phone call from a long-time church associate. Over the years we have had numerous occasions to work together on projects related to our United Methodist annual conference. Assuming she was calling to talk about some church matter, I was only mildly surprised to hear her voice that morning. My surprise quickly turned to sadness.

She had called to talk to me about a piece I had written for our conference newspaper, expressing my views about the importance of doctrine for the church. (I had written out of concern for the opinion that doctrine divides, therefore we should avoid it. I don't think we can.) My friend told me she appreciated my opinion and wanted to use the article in her Sunday school class. First she needed to check something.

I could hear the tension and hesitance in her voice. She wanted to know if I was a "member" of a certain (she named the group) conservative organization well known in United Methodism and perceived among moderates and liberals as harshly right wing.

"Ah, here we go," I thought to myself. I asked her how my associations with this group affected her using my little article. Her answer boiled down to the implication that my reputation had sunk in her estimation and, in a sense, I was now disqualified from having an opinion worth a hearing by folks like her. She was too polite to say it that bluntly, but it was clearly what she meant. I sensed that she felt a little betrayed, hence my sadness. We have known each other a long time and I have prided myself on being open and candid about my opinions on some of the highly contentious issues facing our church. Evidently it had been OK for me to hold such views as long as I didn't associate with "the wrong" organizations.

I'm still pondering that tone in her voice. It was not what one would expect between two people who recognized their differences but knew a deeper connection as brother and sister in Christ. No, sadly, it seemed more like my friend had begun to think of me as an adversary – even "the enemy." We talked further about her specific concerns (some of them so stereotypical about "conservative" conspiracies that, were these matters not so painful, they would be humorous), but that fearful tone overshadowed everything. I will long remember the heaviness I felt after that phone call.

An isolated incident? Not at all. In the past few months I have participated in two dialogues and numerous private conversations over two recently published books touching on United Methodism. The first, by Bishop Joseph Sprague (*Affirmations of a Dissenter*), describes his convictions on issues significantly affecting the church. His most contentious claims – for people like myself – touch on the nature and authority of the Bible and the significance of Jesus Christ for the world's salvation. The second book, by Leon Howell (*United Methodism@Risk*), purports to describe the sinister influence of a number of "right-wing" groups in the United Methodist Church. I have had associations with three of the groups he mentions as dangerous to the church.

The pastor who organized a couple of these dialogues is so up in arms about the "conservative" take-over of the church that she has sold more than forty copies of *United Methodism@Risk* in her congregation. I had read the book, so I was eager to join in the dialogue, because there is much to refute — blatant inaccuracies and misleading suggestions, stuff that's hard for a conservative to take.

Not much dialogue took place, however; mostly speeches and questions aimed at me about what the groups (mentioned in Howell's book) thought they were doing. For example, one person asked, "Why are these groups so interested in the United Methodist Church?" I was puzzled by the question: "these groups" are made up of United Methodists. They fall into the category of "caucuses" that Ken Rowe at Drew University lists in his resource, *United Methodist Studies: Basic Bibliographies.* There are numerous such groups associated with United Methodism which have no official status, meaning they receive no denominational funding. Obviously they must raise money to promote their opinions - exactly what Leon Howell and the United Methodist Information Project did to fund the book they published. Again the irony: we're sitting in a "dialogue" talking in suspicious tones about organizations' funding methods while reading a book published from funds raised in the same way.

No matter. The real point, for most of the discussants, was that these "outsiders" are unfairly and unjustly trying to influence the United Methodist Church in a bad direction. They're big, they're rich, they're powerful, they're harsh and uncompassionate. No one openly made these remarks. It came through in the tone of voice and the questions. "Conservative" is shorthand word for "rich, powerful and mean." And anyone who does not share the "conservative agenda" should be afraid. The Howell book is especially good at stirring up fear. It's a strange feeling to talk to people who think that if folks like me manage to gain too much influence in the church, we will do great damage. I know this feeling is not limited to one side of the divide. Still, it's a strange feeling.

In view of these experiences, I want to explain why I think that fear — in this case of conservatives — is such a prevalent emotional undertone for liberals in our denomination. Certainly fear is not a feeling only liberals have these days. I've heard - more than I care to admit - those strident screeches from conservatives bemoaning the liberal sell-out of the church. As a conservative, however, I am concerned about the kind of fear I think I have noticed in these recent conversations. And I would like to try to analyze it and at least in part try to lay it to rest.

Before I make my points, however, let me first define these terms that we say we hate, but use anyway. 'Conservatives' believe that there is an enduring and necessary doctrinal core that serves to identify and give shape to the Church. This irreducible core can be re-stated and updated for each generation, but only in ways that maintain continuity with the tradition. (I realize that even this idea is subject to debate, since liberals believe that they, too, are maintaining contact with the tradition. This is one of the big bones of contention between us.) Conservatives typically refer to the Nicene and Apostles Creeds as normative summaries of Christian teaching.

Only occasionally do people, in the heat of debate, acknowledge that conservatives value tolerance and inclusiveness. Usually they get mentioned only in relation to liberal causes. Conservatives are committed to tolerance both as a value and as a practical matter, to loving their neighbors every bit as much as liberals are committed to such aims. We believe in these values, but think that they should not blunt the sharp corners of core doctrines for the sake of some vague notion of inclusiveness.

I understand "liberals" to be primarily concerned with making the Christian faith understandable, credible and relevant to the present world. Liberals believe that "faith and love" (experience and attitudes) take precedence over doctrine, since doctrines are understood to be secondary, culture- and time-bound formulations. People ("conservatives") are foolish to place too much emphasis on crystallized statements from the past.

Conservatives often do not recognize liberals' interest in doctrine. Theologically liberal people have definite ideas about the nature and purposes of God in the world. Even though they may prefer to talk of religious or spiritual experience rather than doctrine, certain concepts of God are constantly active. In other words, their vision of God's nature drives their commitment to love and justice. In fact, it is precisely doctrine that becomes the point of conflict with conservatives. Liberals think of themselves as progressive in doctrine and, conversely, they think of conservatives as stuck in the past.

This notion (of progress) could not be more aptly illustrated than by Marcus Borg's most recent book, *The Heart of Christianity: Rediscovering a Life of Faith*. Borg goes to some length to write in irenic tones even though he wants to explain why many thinking Christians can no longer abide by orthodox explanations of the faith. He works hard to find non-pejorative terms. It proves to be a game but awkward effort. The conservative position he calls "earlier paradigm." His position, and the one liberals hold, he calls the "emerging paradigm."

For example, on the matter of the Bible, Borg says that "earlier paradigm" Christians believe the Bible is God's Word and take it literally. "Emerging paradigm" Christians read the Bible more contextually, understand the Bible's historical "placed-ness" and grasp its metaphorical qualities. They find meaning in the Bible with guidance from the most recent developments in biblical scholarship. Similar comparisons by Borg touch on other subjects, such as the nature and work of Jesus Christ.

I'll have to let pass the temptation to refute his facile and maybe even disingenuous comparisons. Suffice it to say that "earlier paradigm" Christians always come out badly in this book. To be sure, he acknowledges that they are sincere people with an authentic faith. They're just ill informed (he doesn't say it this sharply, he just lets the reader figure it out) about matters such as the true nature of the Bible and the best methods for properly understanding it. The point that interests me the most is this idea of progress so strongly implied in his descriptive terms – "earlier" and "emerging." It is impossible to miss the inference: emerging paradigm Christians are progressive. It is not a big step from "progressive" to "fresh, growing, open to the future." "Emerging paradigm Christians" continue the search. They are being liberated from the past's shackles. They're always on the cutting edge.

Earlier paradigm Christians are not. For whatever reasons, they are stuck in the past, clinging to a world that no longer exists. The suggestion Borg makes is the same one that surfaces in conversations between liberals and conservatives. I am constantly struck by how often the idea of progress arises and the manner in which it does. The scenario typically goes something like this: whenever someone raises a thorny doctrinal question, particularly if it is in reference to a traditional understanding of Jesus' nature and work or the authority of the Bible, participants quickly default to telling their stories, sharing their faith journeys as a way of explaining how they have "moved past" such beliefs. They have, in short, progressed.

There is a connection between this mindset and why there seems to be a lot of fear between liberals and conservatives. There must be some reason why we conservatives don't "get it," in other words, why we don't see these matters in the same way, why we don't draw the same conclusions. Maybe we haven't gotten a very good education. Maybe we're just not yet very well informed. We probably haven't read the right books. Maybe we just don't yet understand, but with time we will. In that case, there's still hope. We can keep reading and talking with our more enlightened liberal friends and "get it" eventually.

If it were a matter of lack of understanding, however, I don't think fear would be the tone I've heard so often lately in my conversations. I would not have heard it in my friend's voice in that phone call. 'Pity' would better name it. But it doesn't. It is fear, grounded in the usually-unspoken question: "How is it that you manage to keep believing things that we (and all thinking people) simply can no longer believe?"

Maybe we do it for (cynical) political reasons. That would be reason to fear. But the more frightening possibility is that the answer may be psychological. Maybe we conservatives cling to old ideas because of some sort of need. We can't deal very well with the present, pluralistic world, so we try to nail everything down, clarify who's "in" and who's "out." We package our moral and theological absolutes and then start kicking out anyone who disagrees with us. Maybe we conservatives are driven by fear. Frightened people with power can do frightening things, like "turn the clock back on women," a concern my friend raised in our phone conversation. She actually thinks we're trying to prevent women from entering ministry, a concern I have heard more than once from my liberal friends.

As long as people who think of themselves as liberal refer to this psychological explanation for why we conservatives stick to our guns, we will never have a serious dialogue. You will always be able to attribute our ideas to something less rational, more sinister. But we have reasons – good ones – for thinking the way we do.

And we want to talk with you about those reasons. We understand that you don't agree with us. We're OK with that prospect. We just want you to take our ideas seriously, to listen to us explain ourselves without constantly filtering everything through that fear.

Disagree with us. Criticize us. Oppose us at General Conference. Just don't fear us.

BLESSING SAME-SEX UNIONS

| Why churches should and could |

Randall Tremba (2002)

Dear Pastor,
I am struggling with a statement you made in church a few Sundays ago. You said that you believed same-sex unions should be blessed by the church. Could you direct me to Scripture passages that would help me to understand the basis for your statement? I would appreciate any help you can give me.
Thank you.
Stephen (not actual name)

Dear Stephen,
Thank you for asking me about this difficult issue. I am grateful for your concern. I too have struggled with this matter for many years. For many people, the Bible isn't even a factor in this issue. But, obviously, for you and me (and many others) it is. For better or worse, the Bible

has a knack for stirring up warm conversations about a lot of interesting matters and that's probably a pretty good thing overall.

Many mainline churches (Methodists, Episcopalians, Lutherans, Southern Baptists, and Presbyterians) held national conventions this summer. All of them, in one way or another, passed resolutions banning their pastors from blessing same-gender unions. Proponents and opponents of the bans cited the Bible to support their positions. What's going on here?

In the past 50 years or so, many of us have been learning to read and respect the Bible in a different way — less as a superstitious totem full of absolute answers to all of life's questions and more as a dynamic and multifaceted witness to God's revelation through Jesus Christ and the Holy Spirit. We are reclaiming the Bible from 18th-century (Enlightenment) literalism that attempted — from two extremes — to "make sense" of the Bible by finding scientific explanations for every miracle or by reading it as flat prose rather than a tapestry of myth, lore, story, poetry, proverbs, and gospel. I think you'd agree that God's language (however expressed) would be at least as complex, profound, richly layered, interesting, and occasionally ambiguous as our own.

Some of us are reclaiming the Bible as a witness to the living word and wisdom of God. We are listening to both the text and the Spirit. We are learning to take into account experience, reason, tradition, and the insights of the community in which we live and pray.

Currently there are two basic "schools" or methods of interpreting the Bible. Those who hold and practice these different methods are sincere, conscientious, and thoughtful people and deserve our respect. Both methods are present in most churches, including ours. They are competing schools and not readily compatible. (They are similar to the two different ways that Supreme Court Justices interpret the Constitution.) One method is more literal than the other. The other is more contextual than literal. I grew up in the first school but now work within the second.

I once would have opposed (based on the Bible) churches blessing same-gender unions. Now I favor it. Where in the Bible, you ask, is there any support for that?

First, to begin plainly, let me say that there is no single verse or passage in the Bible that clearly approves or encourages a blessing of same-gender unions. In fact, several verses flatly disapprove. Those of us (quite a few, but still a minority) who have come to this conclusion (blessing same-gender unions) do so by a series of interpretive steps.

While confessing that the Bible is the church's unique repository of divine wisdom, those of us in the "contextual school" nonetheless believe that it must be carefully and reverently interpreted in light of contemporary knowledge and experience. We begin by reading the Bible as best we can out of its original context (its Hebrew and Greek languages; its cultural and historical settings); we try to discern between cultural "husks" and the essential "kernel"; we consider the history of diverse traditional interpretations and understandings; and we pray (alone and in fellowship with others) in order to discern the living word of Christ, which speaks afresh to the churches.

The gospel of John puts these words on Jesus' lips: "I have much to tell you but you can't bear it all now. I will send my Spirit who will lead you into truth." (John 16:12-13)

If we are quiet, humble, and attentive, we just may hear the Spirit speak. We may be led into truth. It wouldn't be the first time.

There are clear precedents for new interpretive steps even in the first-century church. At that time God's written word (for example, Leviticus) clearly required circumcision as a sign of inclusion in the covenant community of faith (Judaism). But with the sudden entrance of uncircumcised "gentiles" into the "Jesus movement," the church (Peter, Paul, James, et al) gathered to discuss the new situation. The church made a concession: circumcision would be optional for the gentiles. (Acts 15)

What?! Modify God's ancient, written law? Unheard of!

That "concession" is now a glorious affirmation of the gospel of Jesus Christ.

A few centuries ago, churches (especially the European Catholic church) resisted (and even persecuted people over) the discoveries of Galileo and Darwin by citing specific Bible verses to refute a "sun-centered" solar system and the biological processes of evolution.

Eventually, in the light of scientific findings, the Bible was re-read and the churches discovered that these scientific findings were not incompatible with the essential truth of the Bible. In fact, we learned to stand in greater, not lesser, awe of God's fantastic creation.

For many centuries the Bible was cited by most churches to keep women in subordination to men. Women were not allowed to speak in churches or to be ordained to ministry. Furthermore, because Jesus and Paul never clearly condemned slavery, Africans were kept in slavery in America and elsewhere. But because of the "cries of the oppressed" the church re-read the Bible and discovered that some portions of the Bible were culturally conditioned and not part of the essential truth of redemption. In other words, some parts of the Bible were given higher value than others.

Just a few decades ago, divorced persons were not allowed to remarry in the church or receive the church's blessing. Some churches — the Roman Catholic and some Baptists, for example — citing verses from the Bible, still refuse to bless a second marriage. But many other churches re-visited the scriptural taboos against divorce and remarriage and interpreted them in the light of other, more prominent teachings about forgiveness and redemption. With so many divorces and remarriages in society (and in the church), churches made another concession: better to acknowledge such marriages and provide some kind of official covenantal structure, support, and blessing (in part, to mitigate the temptations to promiscuity) than to ignore them and condemn them to "life outside the church."

That "concession" has now become an affirmation of God's redemption.

Those are some of the precedents that underlie my conviction that the church could and should provide covenantal structure, support, and blessing to same-gender unions — to encourage fidelity and to mitigate the temptations to promiscuity, which is deadly in the gay community. Such a conviction is based on new understandings of sexuality that simply were not available to ancient Israel and the first-century church just as Galileo's and Darwin's discoveries were not.

There is enough scientific evidence (though it is not conclusive) to suggest that most homosexuals do not choose to be that way. With so much social stigma and persecution against homosexuals in nearly all societies, I can't imagine many voluntarily choosing that "option." Our sexual orientation (which, as you know, is very powerful) seems to be fixed and virtually irreversible by age five. It seems that about two to five percent of the human population (and some animals as well) fall near the homosexual end of the sexuality continuum through no "fault" of their own or their parents.

Now, because we are sinful (or, should I say fearful?) people, we (in whatever majority we are) tend to exclude and persecute whom we consider odd and "dirty" people. But Jesus clearly went out of his way to include and bless those whom society excluded. To be sure, there is no specific instance of Jesus doing that for a known homosexual. But there's enough precedent for what he did do in his cultural setting that I feel certain that it is his voice (the Spirit) speaking in and to the churches in this surprising (and troublesome) way.

Is it not time for churches to make another concession and embrace a glorious affirmation of the living, loving gospel?

There's more that could be said here. But maybe that is enough for now. This matter is very much on my mind and heart. We have more than a few homosexuals and parents of homosexuals in our congregation. This is not an abstract issue by any means for me and especially not for them! Religious words speak loudly and religious symbols even louder.

I welcome the opportunity to hear more about how you feel and think about this matter. I have great admiration for people who struggle to discern God's way in order to better love and care for all God's children.

Sincerely,
Randy

CREATIVE INTENTIONS

| When 'mob rule' ethics sublimate personal morality |

John Lane Denson (2010)

SOME ETHICISTS CONTEND THAT THE DIFFERENCE between ethics and morals can seem somewhat arbitrary, but that there is one, albeit a subtle difference. subtle escapes me, especially whenever I try it myself, but it is helpful for me to search for such a difference in the creative intentions of our nation's founders.

Morals define personal character. Ethics stress a social system in which those morals are applied. Ethics point to standards or codes of behavior expected by the group to which the individual belongs. This could be national ethics, social ethics, company ethics, professional ethics, political ethics, or even family ethics. So while a person's moral code is more or less fixed as conscience, the ethics he or she practices can be other-dependent.

Some recent commentary on the current health care situation — which seems never over despite President Obama having signed the legislation – compares the new law to the 1964-65 Civil Rights Act. One commentator viewed health care legislation alongside the Civil Rights Act as a "moral imperative" gradually fulfilling the creative intentions of a democracy, that is, of our founders and of the Constitution they gave us. Such a viewpoint certainly must be especially frustrating for those who haven't yet got over civil rights or even women's suffrage; their numbers seem to remain legion.

Criminal defense lawyers, for example, must frequently contend with the difference between ethics and morals. The lawyer's personal moral code likely finds murder immoral and reprehensible, but ethics demand that the accused client be defended as vigorously as possible, even when the lawyer knows the party is guilty and he or she also surmises that a freed defendant potentially could lead to more crime. Legal ethics must override personal morals for the greater good of upholding a justice system. Such a system holds that the accused have the right to a fair trial in which the prosecution must prove guilt beyond a reasonable doubt.

The prosecution and court also must deal with the difference between ethics and morals. In some cases, past actions of the accused might resonate with the current charge, but are kept out of evidence so as not to prejudice the jury. In a sense, the prosecutor "lies by omission" in representing the case, never revealing the prejudicial evidence. The same prosecutor, however, would likely find it reprehensible to fail to tell a friend if her date had a potentially dangerous or suspect history.

Another area in which ethics and morals can clash is at the workplace, where company ethics can play against personal morality. Corporate greed that blurs its own ethical lines, when coupled with unreasonable time demands, can lead to an employee's dilemma: having to chose between a stressful, demanding and consuming work ethic and family moral obligations to spouse and children. Conversely, people lose jobs every day because of poor personal morals such as employee theft, a common reason for dismissal.

Abortion is legal and therefore medically ethical, and some find it personally immoral. Fundamentalists, extremists, and even mainstream theists all have different ideas about morality that affects each of our lives, even if indirectly through social pressures or legal discrimination. Many believe homosexuality is morally wrong, yet some of these same people also believe it is unethical to discriminate against the civil rights of homosexuals as a group. These are plain examples of ethics and morals in contention.

So maybe there is a moral imperative. Maybe there is a point at which the command to love our neighbors becomes abrasive for Christians. Groups of neighbors (i.e., society, Congress, political parties, or other institutions) can safely ignore their neighbors, even groups of neighbors, who need health care. Not being able to love like individuals can, groups must realize that in our society it is justice that is the social equivalent of love. Of course, government cannot mandate that we love one another, but it can and must order and establish a just society.

The Church is one place where individuals can and should learn about the difference between morality and ethics, and how the latter can undermine the former. The Church can be a place where we can see and experience how the interplay of morality and ethics has changed throughout biblical history – what my church, the Anglican Communion, has called its normative tradition and to which it ascribes primary authority along with tradition and reason. The Church is a community where liturgy should shape both morality and ethics, since in our faith communities we seek to know and approach God's will for humanity's well being.

Mob rule severely illustrates how personal morals can be sublimated when the ethic of the mob takes over. Be they political parties or so-called Christian militia groups, such organizations can camouflage their members so that an individual's morality doesn't get so embarrassingly exposed. This is where our prophetic ministry to indict our evils joins with our pastoral commission to love and to work for the just peace of society. Such a society encompasses our individual selves, our congregations, and all the systems to which God calls us. Perhaps that is our moral imperative, if seen only through a glass darkly.

perSPECtive
perspective

perspecTive
perspectiVe

Perspective

PERspective

THE HARDENING OF AMERICA
J. Philip Wogaman (2003)

IN A RECENT SPEECH AT TEXAS A&M, National Security Advisor Condoleezza Rice sought to explain the implications of 9/11 for current U. S. policy in the world: "We are now engaged in trying to harden the country." She explained that "that means thinking about airport security, visa requirements, protection of nuclear power plants, and other physical and cyber infrastructure." She further declared that "if we are to remain who we are—open and trusting and free—we cannot harden the country enough to fully protect ourselves."

There may be enough ambiguity in these remarks, taken in context, to preserve them from the most negative ethical connotations that leap to mind. But, in the context of actual administration policy, the word "harden" has to do with more than physical security arrangements found to be necessary after 9/11. Our attitudes toward the world, and particularly toward our adversaries, had to be hardened. Thus, we should use force where necessary, and where there is doubt about what is necessary, we should never resolve that doubt by trusting in weaker or softer alternatives.

When in doubt about a foreigner's potentiality as a terrorist, that person should be kept in custody until the doubt is removed. When in doubt about whether Iraq possessed weapons of mass destruction, evidence that it did should be trusted even if the evidence was not entirely definitive. When in doubt about whether such weapons could be located or their use at least contained, a war should be mounted "to disarm Saddam," rather than trusting in UN inspectors. When in doubt about whether the world community would unite around use of force, the United States and a "coalition of the willing" should proceed unilaterally. When in doubt about the UN's capability of establishing an interim authority in post-war Iraq, the United States (and the coalition) should use its obvious power to make sure the job is done right. We do not know how much further the hardened U.S. policy is prepared to go in forcibly challenging other regimes such as Iran, North Korea and Syria.

Above all, we do not want to be or appear to be soft! I am reminded of Machiavelli's advice to the Prince on the question, is it better for a ruler to be loved or to be feared? Machiavelli, never prone to give a soft answer, replied that, while "we should wish to be both" loved and feared, "since love and fear can hardly exist together, if we must choose between them, it is far safer to be feared than loved." His reason is that people in general are "thankless, fickle, false, studious to avoid danger, greedy of gain, devoted to you while you are able to confer benefits upon them...but in the hour of need they turn against you."

Machiavelli defended the morality of his hardness by citing the example of Cesare Borgia who "was reputed cruel, yet his cruelty restored Romagna, united it, and brought it to order and obedience; so that if we look at things in their true light, it will be seen that he was in reality far more merciful than the people of Florence, who, to avoid the imputation of cruelty, suffered Pistoja to be torn to pieces by factions." One wonders whether Joseph Stalin and Saddam Hussein were students of this version of morality, for neither could be accused of excessive softness, and both of them similarly confronted problems of factional and ethnic disunity.

It would appear that we are well advanced toward the hardening of America. Soft versions of internationalism, including ideals of global community, are not going to receive much leadership from this nation. Our military power and our will to use it, unilaterally and even preemptively, have now been well demonstrated; that will be greatly respected if not feared. If our power is also resented, a hardened America can expect to get along anyway. In the end, it is the power itself that is decisive.

Nor is the hardening of America limited to international relations. In respect to crime, the dominant popular and political consensus is that the worse thing is to be too soft. Thus, a substantial (though perhaps slightly diminishing) majority of the American people continues to support the death penalty, and harsh prison terms (including the "three strikes and you're out" laws) ensure an ever-increasing prison population.

In economic matters we've decided that the best way to deal with poverty is to make sure the welfare programs are not too generous, and, so far as corporations are concerned, there should be as few restraints as possible. If a worker has to be laid off after 30 years of faithful service, then management should not get sentimental about this needful decision. In politics itself, the conventional wisdom in both parties is that 30- second attack ads are the surest way to drive one's opponent's poll numbers down, and if it works that is the only relevant consideration.

What shall we make of this hardening of America? Let us acknowledge that there is a place for hardheaded realism in the life of community. We have to have a police force. We have to defend the country when attacked. We ought to be willing to stop genocide and despotism. But how far are we really willing to go in the direction of Machiavelli's assessment of human nature? Sin there is, aplenty; the doctrine of original sin is an irrefutable theological insight. But sin is not the last word in the Christian vocabulary. That would be grace. And if, with Wesley, we believe in prevenient grace, we can acknowledge the presence of God and of goodness everywhere. The reality of sin makes realism, including some uses of force, necessary. The presence of God and of grace means we can also trust in deeds and policies based upon kindness and a spirit of community.

As I write these words, Christians are preparing for the observances of Good Friday and Easter. The events these observances commemorate illustrate the incredible power of God and of love, not operating through human hardness but through what appears to be weakness. Jesus, crucified as a common criminal, "despised and rejected," exemplifying on the cross an unimaginable quality of love, and setting loose a power in human affairs that a Machiavelli could scarcely imagine.

We are warned in Scripture about the spiritual perils of hardness of heart. Judged harshly by Pharisees for healing a man on the Sabbath, Jesus "was grieved at their hardness of heart" (Mark 3:5). Commenting on the easy dismissal of wives by husbands, authorized in Mosaic law, Jesus said "Because of your hardness of heart he wrote this commandment for you" (Mark 10:5). In Ephesians we are told that we must no longer be like those who "are darkened in their understanding, alienated from the life of God because of their ignorance and hardness of heart" (4:18). Second Corinthians speaks of how the glory of God was hidden from those "whose minds were hardened" (3:14). Hebrews calls upon Christians to "exhort one another every day, as long as it is called 'today,' so that none of you may be hardened by the deceitfulness of sin" (3:13). Alongside these admonitions, there is a host of words encouraging us to be kind and gentle in spirit, loving and caring for one another, even to the point of loving our enemies.

Is that an ethic designed only for Christians in the bosom of the community of faith? Is it suitable only as an "interim ethic" in expectation of the end of the age? Will it "work" in the institutions and policies of society, where many different kinds of sinners and saints must get along? Is it anything more than soft sentimentality when ventured on the global level where special perils lurk and human unkindness is expressed with formidable power?

We have, even in the incredible wickedness and bloodshed of the past century, witnessed extraordinary embodiments of love and justice in movements to overcome oppression and in the policies of compassionate states.

It would, I think, truly be sentimental to say there is no place at all for the forcible restraint of evil in this sinful world. And yet it is worse than sentimental to become so hardened as to regard force as the main basis of institutional life and policy formulation. The bonds of life in community are and must be deeper than that.

I yearn for an America that is a lot less hardened in its approach to social problems, and I dream of a world in which the leadership of this land is an embodiment of the hopes of humankind.

PROCEDURAL JUSTICE AND BIBLICAL JUSTICE
Heidi Hadsell (2006)

WE AMERICANS ARE QUITE ATTACHED to our ideas of justice. Indeed, it is often our shared ideas, if not of justice itself at least of procedural justice, that unite us more than almost anything else.

We teach our children to obey the umpire and that what is important—win or lose—is how they play the game. The dominant moral metaphor in much of American life, one that comes from the sports field and gets applied to many other areas of life, especially business, has become that of the "level playing field" upon which fair competition is said to take place.

Indeed, for many Americans, large inequalities in income, the professions, housing and the like, that might be morally questionable are easily made tolerable with the assurance that, at the start of, or inherent in, what is imagined as the competition (wherever that is deemed to be, in whatever sphere of life) the positions were roughly equal. Yes, many will concede, the outcomes are widely disparate, but since the procedures were followed and were in themselves fair, the results are just.

How then do we North American Christians respond to the substantive ideas of justice that we find in the gospels?

What do we think for instance of the text about the laborers and the householder who pays the same wages to those who have worked in the fields all day as he pays to those who have worked several hours or even less? This equal payment for unequal amounts of work, from the perspective of procedural justice, seems simply unfair and antithetical to our common ideals of justice.

And yet, this is a text that is compelling precisely because it challenges many of our ideas of justice and teaches us about the up-ended logic of the kingdom of God. What do we make of this story, which we find in Matthew 20:1-16?

IN THE FIRST PLACE, AT LEAST FROM MY PERSPECTIVE, the depiction of the work life of common laborers in the biblical text virtually erases the 2000 years between this text and the world we live in today. There they are, a group of men early in the morning, gathered on a corner or in an empty lot, waiting, hoping to be picked for a day of work in the vineyards. They are all unskilled laborers with only the strength of their bodies with which to earn a livelihood. The lucky ones get picked and are off to work for the day. The unlucky ones wait. They are still there several hours later. They need the job. And they are still there towards the end of the day, unwilling perhaps to go home to a hungry family with empty hands.

There I was a few weeks ago, early one weekend morning on my way into Manhattan. I pulled into one of the towns off the Saw Mill Parkway looking for coffee. And there they were, 40 or 50 men, mostly Latinos I guessed, on a street corner huddled against the cold, waiting for someone to come by and choose them for a day of labor. Just like 2,000 years ago, some would get lucky and others wouldn't. And the unlucky ones would wait there on the corner just as the Mexican day laborers I saw as a child in rural California, just as they do today in rural and urban places across the country, and just as they did in Palestine 2,000 years ago.

Every time I read this text I wonder whom Jesus was addressing.

Imagine, choosing this example of generosity to day laborers so low in the order of things that they are virtually invisible to society—temporary workers, with all they have to offer being their brute strength. The answer to the question of whom Jesus was addressing has to be, first, that this was a common occurrence and thus a good example from which to teach everyone. Second, and more importantly, while Jesus was addressing all of us, those who could most readily see the possibilities and imagine the joy of the kingdom of God and the God's miraculous generosity were (and are) those with lives like the day laborers who were not picked for work or picked only late in the day.

Although I am ashamed to say it, I know for sure that, were I one of the laborers picked early and had worked in the hot sun all day, I would be furious at the householder who paid the last to arrive the same as he paid me. That's the point, right? Who wouldn't be angry?

And yet, the householder sees it from another perspective. He is thinking of being fair to the ones who worked in the fields all day, but he also is thinking of the ones who, although they didn't work all day, still have needs, still have families to feed. Thinking in this way requires a new approach to justice or to fairness. And it is with this new take, this new perspective, that Jesus subverts the prevailing logic. He turns it from a zero-sum game in which, if one person wins another has to lose, to a different logic altogether: "I am doing you no wrong. Am I not allowed to do what I choose with what belongs to me? Or, do you begrudge me my generosity?"

THIS STORY IS ONE OF THE INSTANCES in which Jesus critiqued established truths and the established morality of the reigning common sense. And he did so from a more substantive and less formal morality, with a horizon beyond that of human history. It was an alternative ethic that he recommended and taught, demonstrating on the one hand how limited, how small-minded and how cramped much of our actual morality is and, on the other hand, showing the possibilities of living another way. This, of course, just drove others crazy, especially those who were in a position to benefit from the way things were—like the day laborers who were first in the field, or other householders taking advantage of the cheap wages flowing from the surplus of laborers looking for jobs.

What an interesting story to reflect on in a season in which the United States is engaged in a loud and contentious debate over immigration. The story won't solve the immigration questions, which are very complex. But it does invite one to consider whether there isn't a sense in which, morally, the immigration debate boils down to this:

Like the day laborers, there are those of us who got lucky and, in effect, got work first, generations ago perhaps or perhaps more recently; and there are those of us who have only very recently arrived, within the last decade or so, and not always through the means of legal immigration permits.

ARE NOT MANY OF US, LIKE THE DAY LABORERS, complaining bitterly that the recent arrivals are receiving the same wages as we are? And is not Jesus insisting in response that we think again, that we understand that from the perspective of the kingdom there is another logic, another morality? This is a morality of openness and inclusion, a morality of generosity, in the light of which we can see that we are all different, perhaps in very many ways, but, at the end of the day, we are very much alike. We all need work, and we all need to feed our families, to be in community, to be a part of some place, some civic order. Decency to the latecomers need not imply that those there earlier do not get their due.

But in this text, Jesus is not only talking about an alternative morality in the light of the kingdom of God. He is also saying something about faith or the quest for faith. Faith and faithfulness are not a question of who got there first. The late arrivals, those who only recently have come or have only now been grasped by faith, or those who are in the first tentative steps of the journey, are, according to the logic of the kingdom of God, at no disadvantage whatsoever to those who are already there. God cares for all. Faith is a participatory activity, something we can all engage in whether we come early or late, no matter who we are or where we are in our journey.

Faith is not about rules. Or, better stated, faith transforms human rules, practices and perspectives, since faith is related to God and God's abundance and generosity, and not to where we are in the human pecking order.

TITANIC CHRISTIANITY

| The peril of holding out on God |

Steven Blackburn (2009)

THE NEWS IS OUT. As reported by the Associated Press September 28, 2009, "Religious life won't be the same after downturn." American churches are feeling the effects of the current economic situation no less than other sectors of our society. Money is short, volunteerism is contracting as people scramble for jobs that pay, and smaller churches, especially, are feeling the squeeze. Having pastored two small congregations in rural Connecticut from 1981 to 2001, and now volunteering gratis as the organist in a third, I have seen first-hand the precarious situation in which many churches find themselves. Just this past year our pastor's compensation was halved.

Of course, worrying about backwoods churches is not at the top of the list for many people today, and closing the doors of a small church might not be mourned as much as shutting down a rural post office, disbanding a volunteer fire department, or dissolving a local cemetery association, leaving headstones to fall into disrepair as grass, brush, moss, and mold take their toll.

Still, whenever a rural church can no longer serve its community, the effects are there. My denomination recently closed one of our Connecticut churches, which sold off the building and grounds to the town historical society. The local newspapers carried the story, but sometimes such news slips by, and only when there is a need does the truth present itself, the truth that there is no longer a local body of believers to minister to the poor, the hungry, the sick, the bereaved, or the outcast.

This reminds me of the familiar proverbial story about a man who had a new house. Two cars and a bright, shiny boat filled his garage. A color television, a Super-Nintendo, and a computer screen gleamed in his den. His family was healthy.

His custom – when he was in town... when the fish weren't biting... when he was not on the beach or at the lake... when he had no guests... when he had nothing else to do -- was to go to church. When he attended, he spent his time deploring the decaying state of the congregation: Sunday school participation was low, their choir scanty, the attendance small, the offerings poor. "They ought to do better," he said. "What do they think religion is all about, anyways?"

Many vacations and days off came, and went. According to the way of the world, this man's children grew up. They did not go to church. The reason, their father said, was that the people down at the church had not kindled his children's interest in religion. Then the man's health failed, and he noticed something strange. Those people down at the church no longer came by. He was in the hospital and they did not visit him. And lo, he was very angry.

"Where is the church?" he demanded. "Oh," somebody said, "that church closed its doors long ago." "You're kidding," the man cried. "THEY should never have let it die!"

The man in this little parable, if we can call it that, practiced an extreme form of what I call "Titanic Christianity." Titanic Christianity is found everywhere, in every denomination, in every congregation. And in case you get the wrong idea, Titanic Christianity even afflicts those of us who attend a bit more regularly than the man in our parable.

For Titanic Christianity only sees the tip of the iceberg. For some, the tip of the iceberg is a church which is available for weddings, baptisms, and funerals. For others, the tip of the iceberg is a faith (if you can call it faith) of filling a pew each Sunday morning but not letting anything that happens during the one hour of worship interfere with how they conduct the rest of their life.

Both varieties give the false sensation that somehow your connection with what Paul the Apostle calls the Body of Christ makes you unsinkable. And so our friend sails serenely along in life, looking out above the water level, unmindful that his ship of state not only floats above the water, but ploughs through it, and beneath it, as well. And when the tip of the iceberg is sighted, you give God due, skirting the dangers, while ignoring your other obligations and responsibilities that life, the creation, and the Creator, have laid upon you.

Next thing you know, you're sunk!

NOW A LOT OF PEOPLE PRACTICE TITANIC CHRISTIANITY, saying that is all they are capable of. A more serious variety of following the commands of Christ is left to the Mother Teresa's of this world, or to so-called professional Christians like clergy who are paid, so it is said, to be holy.

This attitude arises from the mistaken conviction that it takes time to practice your faith. Now it *does* take time to perfect it, but that does not mean that you need time off, or a life of leisure, to be a super-Christian, or even just a good one. In fact, the busier you are at living everyday life, the more opportunity you have to give Christianity an opportunity to live itself through you. At the risk of being trite about it, it is a little like whistling while you work. Be a Christian, while you work; far from interfering with your labors, it will help them, and you, along.

But Christianity is not just to be lived for you and your own ends. Quite the contrary, it is to be lived for others, even if the cost to you ends up being great. After all, is that not what Calvary is all about? If you let your faith expand from mere Titanic Christianity, and let it truly live through you, then it will not be long before you recognize the truth so ably put long ago, that "every victory of love over selfishness makes God both real, and lovable, to others."

Otherwise, we are "holding out on God." How are some of the ways in which we do that?

The Prophet Malachi (chapter 3, verses 6-12) voiced the accusation that God's chosen are holding out financially. The situation was this: the crops were poor, income was down, people were feeling the squeeze, and so they were skimping on their tithing – a natural enough, and understandable, sequence of events. What they do not realize is that holding out is not in their best interest, even though in the short run it makes their bank accounts look fatter. Sounds a bit like today, doesn't it? I can even now hear Jesus saying, "Lo, they have their reward." If we are to make room in our lives for God's gifts, we are going to have to give away a few things, making gifts to others.

The Romans had a proverb: "Money is like sea water; the more you drink, the thirstier you become." Is not material wealth like that? You just can't ever have enough. So, just as God was moved to make a gift of God's self at Calvary, let us do the same, remembering that we are created in God's own image.

How else can we hold out on God? There is a person named Ernest, of whom it is said, "He lives in a little world, bounded on the north by Ernest, on the south by Ernest, on the east by Ernest, and on the west by Ernest." This attitude reflects the very reverse of Christianity. Instead of aggressively affirming himself, Ernest should have thought of denying the safe reality of his self-made haven in life. After all, is it not true that only those who dare lose sight of the shore can hope to discover new oceans?

Some would hold out on God by so looking to the life to come, that they would ignore the world of today. Jesus never said that this world was unimportant, but rather that its importance lies not in itself, but in that to which it leads. If we will concentrate on what will last, on what is eternal, then, yes, we will be going against the grain of a society which glories in throwaway diapers, throwaway dishes, and throwaway appliances – maybe you hadn't heard about throwaway appliances? They used to be called durable goods, but now they are built to last only three to five years instead of 25 or more. Planned obsolescence is another word for it. America lives on it. But Christianity calls us to concentrate on the things that will last, and to avoid the shoddy.

Christianity bids us to consider the long term, and not the short. It tells us to seek out the whole picture, instead of just the tip of the iceberg.

The alternative? Well, we who would seek something less than the best shall have our reward. But for those of us who would live for Christ, there is another fate in store.

RONALD REAGAN: A REASSESSMENT
J. Philip Wogaman (2004)

A MONTH OR SO AGO, while waiting in a doctor's office, I happened on a back issue of Time. The magazine, dated September 29, 2003, featured excerpts from the newly published *Reagan: A Life in Letters* (Skinner, Anderson and Anderson, eds., The Free Press). Since the doctor was quite late in getting to me, I had time to absorb a number of the Reagan letters. I found them fascinating.

In order to appreciate my reaction, you have to remember that I have never been a supporter, much less a fan, of the former president. I was hard-pressed to find much in his presidency that I could support. I perceived his mind to be largely vacuous, his policies often mean-spirited. To this day, I have even found it difficult to refer to my city's airport by its new name.

I haven't read the book, but the letters reproduced in Time are enough to make me take a second look. It's not just that he wrote a lot of letters (more than 10,000 have been found), but the sensitivity and openness with which he wrote. Some of the letters are to world-famous figures, some to very ordinary persons, some to family members. Many are very personal in tone. I was struck by the letters to his daughter Patti and son Ron, Jr., for his wise and caring parental advice and his clear commitment to honesty and other important personal virtues. Was he "faking it"? I just don't think so, even though he was famously described as the "great communicator." I could be wrong, but I found the letters I read convincing evidence of greater depth of mind and character than I had previously thought possible.

Then what about his presidency? The letters, at least the ones I read, provided no startling new insights. He was no racist, I'm convinced of that. And yet he rode to power partly on the strength of a California backlash against fair housing legislation and, later, partly on a "southern strategy" catering to racist energies. Early in his administration he fired the late Arthur Flemming as chair of the U. S. Civil Rights Commission.

Dr. Flemming was a member of Foundry Church through most of my tenure there, and I believe there was no one in this country more deeply and wisely committed to civil rights than he was—and he was a Republican, as well. President Reagan did as much as he could to dismantle welfare programs. He lowered taxes, with a tilt in favor of the rich and with the twin effects of starving welfare programs and saddling future generations with huge deficits. All of this (and much, much more) does not demonstrate visionary leadership.

How could the author of those insightful, caring letters have been so shortsighted? In part, it may have been a matter of practical politics, catering to his ultra-conservative political base. But I think it was more than that. He had been a Roosevelt Democrat, voting for FDR all four times. But then he changed. Evidently his experience with Communists (and persons taken to be Communists) in the Screen Actors' Guild had a great effect on him, and he came to regard socialism and anything that smacked of socialism as being of a piece with that.

His anti-Communism was real and deep. When he referred to the Soviet Union as the "evil empire," he was as sincere as he could be. His attitude toward the Soviet Union illustrated a broader tendency to divide the world into good and evil rather more sharply than a realistic view of human life would permit.

Even more: He could not seem to see that society is more than the sum of its individual parts. Personal character is very important, but none of us stands alone. He was, it seems, attracted to the late Ayn Rand, the quintessential individualist. Anybody influenced by her philosophy is almost bound to overlook the ancient Aristotelian insight that human beings are by nature social animals. We are actually, I think, both individual and social by nature. The bonds of fellow humanity are not just matters of convenience and practicality; they are essential to who we are. On the other hand, we are also individual, potentially creative persons. To put this theologically, we stand before God as beloved individuals. But God has also created us in and for community. The practical consequences of this two-sidedness are politically immense.

The task of politics is to establish and maintain conditions that enhance our participation in community. That includes economic well-being, educational opportunity, political rights, freedom of expression, adequate health care, physical security, so far as these things are attainable. The Reagan administration fell very far short.

For all of the acknowledged caring and insight of the Reagan letters, he had so little vision about what a community is and what is needed to sustain its well-being. He saw society as a place of opportunity where "someone can always get rich," overlooking the fact that not all can get rich and neglecting the social effects of vast disparities of income and wealth. As president, he advocated a very limited role for government, severely restricting its ability to deal with economic deprivation. "The taxing power of government must be used," he asserted, "to provide revenues for legitimate Government purposes. It must not be used to regulate the economy or bring about social change. We've tried that and surely must be able to see it doesn't work."

Why dwell on the sometimes enigmatic views of a former president? It is partly to remind ourselves that ethical emphasis must be given both to personal character and to the struggle for the good society, for when we neglect either we diminish both.

It is also to begin to think long thoughts about the current national conversation. For these same issues confront us today, if anything, more than they did during the years of the Reagan administration.

MUSLIMS AS PARTNERS IN INTERFAITH ENCOUNTER: MODELS FOR DIALOGUE

Jane I. Smith (2003)

HARTFORD SEMINARY HAS LONG BEEN DEDICATED to promoting better interfaith understanding in general and, through the work of its Macdonald Center, to Christian-Muslim relations in particular. The mandate of its current president and dean makes dialogue one of the cornerstones of the seminary's pedagogy. Accordingly, the Center has worked to promote and support occasions in which Christians and Muslims come together to learn more about each other, explore theological commonalities and differences, and work for justice in our communities.

Dialogue over the last decade has taken a range of forms, has been initiated for a variety of reasons and has elicited a number of different responses from members of the American Muslim community. It is encouraging to those of us who have worked to foster interfaith conversation to note that, while invitations to talk together until recently have come almost exclusively from Christians to Muslims, the initiative is coming to be shared. Especially since 9/11, Muslims have looked to the dialogue as a necessary part of their endeavor to help explain their religion, to counter rising anti-Muslim prejudices on the part of many Christians and to claim their place as active participants in the American religious scene.

As part of the efforts of the Macdonald Center to encourage Christian-Muslim dialogue in a variety of contexts, I recently engaged a number of American Muslims in conversation about the dialogue, in what ways they find it helpful and how a new agenda might be set for these times in which our religious communities need help and direction in understanding the "other."

This essay highlights one dimension of the many issues that were raised in those conversations, namely the various purposes for which dialogues have been carried out as Muslims have experienced them. From their responses, I have tried to develop a set of models for dialogue. Some of these models have been on the scene for decades while others are just emerging. The naming and descriptions of these categories are my own. I present them here in the hope that they might be useful to churches looking for ways in which to engage their Muslim neighbors in conversation.

Models of Muslim-Christian Dialogue in America

The Confrontation/Debate Model. Debate and confrontation, generally of a theological nature, have characterized Muslim-Christian encounters since the earliest days of Islam. Historically, such encounters were designed not to promote better understanding but to disprove the validity of the other's faith and belief system. Recent immigrants from parts of the world in which tensions between Christians and Muslims are high have experienced this kind of confrontational dialogue and sometimes expect to replicate it here. On the whole, however, debate is not a model that is much appreciated in the American context. It is important, most Muslims say, to get beyond argumentation that fosters an "I am right and therefore you are wrong" attitude.

The Dialogue as Information-Sharing Model. Within a range of different possibilities, this model seems to be the most common form of Muslim-Christian encounter. As Christians become aware of the reality that Islam is the fastest growing religion in America, and that Muslims are increasingly visible in all walks of western life, churches and denominations are recognizing the importance of better understanding their new neighbors. Many Muslims find themselves invited to attend gatherings at which they are asked to talk about the basic beliefs and practices of Islam. They, in turn, may be told about some of the ways in which American Christians observe their own faith. Often a single Muslim is featured as an invited "guest" in a predominantly Christian gathering, thus becoming the focus of Christian attention. One convert to Islam reports that she is often asked to participate in such sessions because she can speak the language of Christians as well as explain Islam. Dialogue is limited in such gatherings to a kind of question-and-answer session, during which participants try to make sure that basic information has been imparted. Many Muslims indicate that they are getting tired of the superficiality of this model. "Such explanatory sessions are frustrating because they are not really dialogue," a Shi'ite woman from Detroit shared with me. "It's time to get down to more serious discussions."

Some Muslims are experiencing a new context for information sharing, however, that they see as a possible model of dialogue. This is the opportunity provided in the college or university classroom, where students from different religious traditions find class discussion as a venue for engaging with each other about faith issues. The fact that many Muslim children are now enrolled in Catholic parochial schools, and that some Christian children go to Muslim schools, suggests the possibility of dialogue at a completely different level. Public schools are also providing opportunities for Muslim children (and often their parents) to talk to other students about their holidays and customs at appropriate times in the Islamic ritual cycle.

The Theological Exchange Model. For a number of years certain Christian groups have encouraged the kind of dialogue in which deeper conversation is held about elements of faith within the traditions of Christianity and Islam. This model has been particularly effective, for example, in the annual regional meetings of the National Conference of Catholic Bishops. Participants in these dialogues, who attend on a regular basis and get to know each other well, exchange perspectives on a number of different theological themes. Some Muslims feel that the theological exchange model is still a very important mode of Muslim-Christian encounter. Others are not so sure, persuaded that this model does not work very well for Muslims because theology is not their primary concern and is not always of great interest to them. Unlike some Christians, Muslims generally do not engage in theological dialogue because they expect to learn something helpful to their own spiritual development. Lurking behind the concerns of some Muslims over this kind of theological exchange is the fear that Christians are subtly using the dialogue forum to continue their efforts at evangelization of Muslims. They worry that Muslims who have had little experience in such theological exchanges will not be prepared to understand what they fear to be the underlying agenda. Most Christians and Muslims who engage in theological dialogue, of course, are quick to affirm that the context should not be one in which judgments are made or persuasion attempted.

The Ethical Exchange Model. Some Muslims have been adamant that the appropriate arena for discussion between Christians and Muslims is not theology but ethics. Concerns for the decline in morality in American society have put ethics on the agenda as a matter of crucial importance for many. In general Muslims express themselves as convinced that, if Christians were to observe the ethical injunctions of their own religion more strictly, many of America's social problems might be alleviated. In any case, they understand that an examination of the ways in which Christians and Muslims can look to the resources of their traditions to provide ethical and moral guidance in the new century would be a profitable endeavor. And as advancements in medical science raise disturbing questions in both communities, some Muslims urge a coming together to share resources and, perhaps, to find common guidance.

The "Dialogue to Come Closer" Model. Proponents of this type of dialogue, both Muslim and Christian, hope that honest conversation among members of the two faiths will identify elements of commonality, leading to a de-emphasis on differences and a re-emphasis on sharing and mutuality. It must be said, of course, that most Muslims are very nervous about this kind of approach, finding it dangerous and expressive of exactly what they most fear about dialogue. We should not, they say, make any moves that will tend to blur the distinctions between our two communities. In its worst form, they believe, such conversations may lead to a kind of syncretism that Christians and Muslims on the whole have tried hard to avoid.

The Spirituality and Moral Healing Model. A small number of Muslims are interested in coming together with Christians for the purpose of pursuing issues of spirituality, or what is sometimes referred to as moral healing. Sometimes this model is associated with an examination of modes of traditional psychology. For others, it means pressing forward together into a deeper form of spiritual experience, which necessitates that participants be at more or less the same "level" of spiritual interest and understanding. Again, most Muslims are not at a point where they are willing to commit themselves to such pursuits and are openly nervous about them.

The Cooperative Model for Addressing Pragmatic Concerns. For many in the American Muslim community the time for talk is over and interest lies in "getting something accomplished together." One person called this the "common enemy" approach – addressing issues that are germane to the wholeness of both groups. It characterizes the attitude of many young people as well as those who have become discouraged at what they feel to be a lack of much progress in dialogue. They feel that it is now time for people of faith to join together in doing community work such as fighting drugs, delinquency and other social ills. Muslims and Christians are working together in several major cities to help resettle Muslim refugees. One of the very practical issues of common concern that is being addressed by a number of the Christian-Muslim dialogue groups around the country is that of intermarriage: how to counsel young people who are contemplating such a marriage, what kinds of support can be offered by the respective communities for couples of mixed faiths, and what concerns should be addressed in terms of the children of such marriages.

Most Muslims and Christians who have been engaged in the

dialogue endeavor agree that dialogue only for the sake of talking tends to be unstructured and unsatisfying. Determining ahead of time, and together, common goals for meeting helps guarantee that results will be helpful for all involved. The models developed above are suggested as a possible way of guiding the planning and preparation of conversations between church and mosque, between Christians and Muslims. They provide a snapshot of "work in progress" as more dialogue efforts develop, and will be enhanced by the contributions of others who begin to develop new models for interaction based on their own experiences.

ON AND ON
Scott Campbell (2001)

MY BROTHER, GLENN, DIED ON JUNE 5, just a bit more than a month shy of his 51st birthday. Lung cancer had spread throughout his body and into his brain, although he remained lucid until the end. Over the subsequent months, I have had an opportunity to claim some of the gifts his living and dying have brought. First, though, let me tell you just a little about who Glenn was.

He remained single all his life, trying his hand at various careers along the way. He served a stint on a nuclear submarine as a sonar technician, but spent the better part of his adult life as a taxi driver, first in Boston and later in Augusta, Maine. During his last few years, he started his own company, Winthrop Taxi, and lived with my parents in their retirement home. On duty he was gregarious and friendly, always doing the little extras like carrying bags of groceries into the homes of the elderly and assisting the inebriated safely into their houses. (It was telling that a bucket left on the bar in one of Winthrop's watering holes during Glenn's illness generated over $600 in contributions.) But on his own time, he was given to more solitary pursuits. He was a gifted driveway mechanic who thought nothing about pulling an engine out of one car and putting it in another (I'll never forget the looks on the faces of one group of parishioners as my family pulled up for our first Sunday at a new church in a car borrowed from Glenn. As I recall it was half Plymouth Fury, half Chevy Belvedere!) Fishing, however, was his passion. He knew all of the best spots within a thirty-mile radius of Augusta.

His preference for time alone sometimes caused hurt feelings among other family members, especially when Glenn would either fail to attend some milestone event, or make a much belated token appearance. All that changed dramatically, however, after he received his diagnosis in November of last year. He couldn't get enough of people. As his pastor, Heidi Chamberlain, put it at his memorial service, Glenn became "a sponge for life." Everyone who crossed his path during the last seven months of his life became a significant encounter for Glenn. He fussed over babies, queried hospital orderlies about their families, was unfailingly good natured with nurses, and couldn't tell his family members enough times how much he loved them and how important their small gestures of kindness were to him.

So, what have I have received out of all this? I would have never expected the first gift Glenn had in mind for us. We were given the gift of laughter. I learned anew of the incredible power of humor to hold the grimmest forces of darkness at bay. Over and over again, Glenn would give us permission to laugh, and in so doing to live, by cracking wise in the most unlikely settings. The day after his second brain operation a nurse came by to ask if she could take his vitals. "As long as you bring them back when you're done" he quipped. When I told him one night that the Red Sox had won and offered the fond hope that this could finally be their year he replied, "No doubt it will be. I've always said they're never going to win it as long as I'm alive." In fact, his last words were a feebly whispered witticism. As my other brother, Stephen, attempted to make him more comfortable, he asked Glenn if his pillow was okay. "Why?" Glenn asked. "Do you want it?" Whenever things became too heavy or sad, Glenn would lift our spirits with the gift of laughter.

The second gift also came as something of a surprise. My dad and I are both clergy, but neither of us could or wanted to be a pastor in that situation. We were the recipients of the ministry of a caring pastor. The loving, totally present and compassionate ministry of Heidi Chamberlain made an unfathomable difference to our whole family. What a gift it was to be ministered to in a time of deep need by a representative of the church of Jesus Christ. Being on the receiving end of effective ministry has strengthened my own sense of calling.

The third gift I take away from Glenn's death is a deepened appreciation for the blessing of family. Stephen and I were with Glenn as he left this life. We held him and kissed him and prayed him into eternity. Stephen climbed into bed with him and held him in his strong arms. We experienced a closeness to one another in sharing those moments that has changed us forever. We are brothers now in a way that we had longed to be, but didn't quite know how.

Finally, I have a deepened regard for the church. All of us, but particularly my parents, were surrounded by loving community, before and after Glenn's death. Food, flowers, gifts, reassuring messages, cards, contributions, warm embraces, tear-brimmed eyes all said in a hundred ways "You are not alone in your grief." I received many messages from colleagues in the weeks following Glenn's death, each one a reminder that I belong to a wonderful family created by virtue of baptism and ordination. I resolve not to take these simple kindnesses for granted, but to return them whenever I can to others in the family. It may be trite to say, but little things do indeed mean a lot.

I haven't told you that Glenn was a volunteer Emergency Medical Technician. He was fearless in his willingness to put himself in danger to aid others. More than once he plunged down into dark ravines to tend to injured accident victims. His colleagues in the Monmouth Rescue Company sounded the last call for his number over the radio at his memorial service. It was followed by complete silence and then the playing of *Amazing Grace* on the bagpipes. In those moments I knew that the work of grace begun in Glenn's life was not over, but would go on and on, visiting places I could not even imagine.

SHARING SACRED HISTORY AND GEOGRAPHY
Yehezkel Landau (2004)

"Zion will be redeemed through justice, and those who return to her through compassion."

— Isaiah 1:27

UNTIL NOW MOST JEWS, CHRISTIANS AND MUSLIMS have been jealous rivals competing for Divine favor. We have been like long-distance runners in a spiritual marathon over centuries, believing that only one competitor could earn the first-place medal while the others would either lose in disgrace or qualify for an inferior prize. How much evil and suffering have been caused by such theological self-glorification?

None of our traditions has been innocent in this regard. We have all succumbed, at one time or another, to spiritual arrogance and blindness. In our present situation, with religious extremism engendering the slaughter of innocents and ideologies to justify such atrocities, we all need to acknowledge our past failings and approach our fellow believers, whose theologies differ from our own, with humility and repentance.

At the Tantur Ecumenical Institute in Jerusalem, where I have taught for many years, Fr. Thomas Stransky resides after serving as rector there. Fr. Tom is an American Paulist priest. He uses a striking metaphor to illustrate the problem of how the three Abrahamic faiths developed in mutual estrangement, each convinced of its own triumphal truth. His image, which I shall embellish a bit, is of a "holy rocket" launched by God to bridge the gap between earth and heaven, between our present woundedness and the fulfilled promise of divine healing.

We Jews believe that the "flight plan" for this holy rocket was revealed at Sinai, as the Israelites journeyed through the wilderness between Egypt and the Promised Land. In this flight plan, revealed in Hebrew, the trajectory takes the Jews from that smoking and thundering mountain into the air, but not outside the earth's gravitational pull (for we Jews are a very down-to-earth, practical people). The rocket travels in a small arc just a few hundred kilometers north and lands in Jerusalem. Jews throughout history have been pilgrims on the road from Sinai to Jerusalem, too often a via dolorosa of suffering for us. But in the messianic future, we reassure ourselves, the rest of humanity will ascend to Jerusalem to join us there, learning Hebrew in an ulpan language course in order to study Torah with us and to appreciate that we were the carriers of the true revelation all along.

Next came Christianity, which proclaimed that a new flight plan had been revealed through Christ, this time in Greek. According to this new understanding, the original rocket launched at Sinai was, in fact, a two-stage vehicle. The first stage, Israel of the flesh, had fulfilled its intended function; but the thrust of Divine energy had now been passed to the second stage of the rocket, the spiritual and true Israel, namely the Church. Moreover, the new flight plan contained a mid-course correction. The rocket's new trajectory took the second stage out of the earth's gravitational field into outer space, where the celestial Jerusalem awaited the pilgrim who wanted to meet the Divine in the devotional heart, not in a particular land or city. The Church declared that one day the whole world would be on board the second stage, including the Jews, and in the meantime those people who chose not to join the Christian fellowship would suffer the consequences of their refusal—either in this world as accursed wanderers, or in the metaphysical realm of hell, or both.

After another six centuries, yet a third monotheistic tradition emerged, this one also laying claim to the earlier prophesies and promises while affirming a new flight plan for the holy rocket. Islam saw itself as the final stage of a three-stage rocket. In the eyes of Muslim believers, the Arabic text of the Holy Qur'an now offered the truest version of the vehicle's trajectory, as global in scope as that of Christianity, but with this-worldly criteria of holiness similar to those of the Jews. On the way to the Day of Judgment, the caliphate on earth would be the realm of Divine dispensation, with the Islamic umma (community) now acting as the vanguard carrier of Divine revelation. According to the new flight plan, Muslims were now at the controls of the rocket, with Jews and Christians already on board as believers to be protected, not condemned, by the dominant Muslim majority. Islam would eventually spread to cover the earth, by persuasion if possible and by force if necessary.

One can argue over which of these flight plans has caused more harm to other communities throughout history. (In my view, this has been largely a matter of political empowerment more than intent). What is undeniable is that all three of the flight plans are self-centered and self-glorifying. Equality among the three faith traditions, grounded in a pluralistic or inclusive theology, is not held out as a goal to be sought. Divine truth and love go together, both limited by some scarcity principle—an odd restriction to ascribe to the Almighty Creator of heaven and earth. At the end of time, according to each of the three faiths, one and only one community will "win" the marathon of sacred history and be vindicated.

This paradigm of exclusive truth and hierarchical dispensation is in need of radical overhaul. If religion is to be a force for good, for life, for blessing, it must undergo a metamorphosis, a real metanoia, and become a force for inclusive, truly unconditional, love. This is not a defense of relativism. It is, instead, recognition of pluralism within the monotheistic family. The one God of History has chosen to reveal the same essential message in different languages or symbol systems, through different messengers at different times. If the adherents of those traditions would focus more on godly (i.e., just and compassionate) behavior toward others, rather than on demonstrating their supremacy over them, surely God's Name would be more genuinely glorified by the faithful and the face of religion would be more attractive to skeptical nonbelievers.

In order to realize this aim, a new paradigm must be found. One Biblical image that could be acceptable to all three monotheistic traditions is that of the rainbow revealed to Noah after the flood, as a sign of the covenant between God and all humanity (whatever sub-covenants may come later). A rainbow is panoply of colors, none more beautiful than another, and the whole spectrum having a beauty greater than that of any single color. And what is the source of this aesthetic wonder? It is the refraction of white light through the prism of the earth's atmosphere.

The parallel for our consideration is this: the "white light" of Divine Truth is refracted through the prisms of historical experience, human language and culture, and subjectivity of thought and feeling. Yet despite these particularities, the general thrust of the Abrahamic faiths is the same: love and serve God through acts of justice and compassion toward other human beings (as well as other creatures). Creed is tested through deed, doctrine through practical discipleship, devotion to God through attending to the needs of our neighbors. Or, as one Hasidic rabbi has taught, "we should care about the welfare of other people's bodies and our own souls, rather than the reverse."

We have to be in constant dialogue with our neighbors in order to know when we might say or do something that is hurtful to them. In our global village, ignorance is no longer an excuse for insensitivity or injury. Before we profess love and concern for them, let us invite our neighbors to tell us what hurts them, so that we can live the Golden Rule with conscious intent, not just pay lip service to it.

To connect this reflection to current events, I will shift my focus from sacred history to sacred geography. I have lived in Israel/Palestine, or the "Holy Land," for 25 years. My home has been in Jerusalem, Al-

Quds to the Muslims. What I have to offer, out of my own faith understanding, is a meditation on what I call the pluralistic geography of Jerusalem. Jews, Christians and Muslims all consider the city to be holy, and they relate to it in iconographic, meta-historical terms. With its four quarters, Jerusalem has been likened to a human heart, with its four chambers. It is indeed a sacred heart, beating to the rhythm of ancient traditions and pumping vitality through the spiritual bodies of all believers in the One God of History. But there are also signs of "cardiac disease" in Jerusalem, with the flow of people and cultural energy from one community to another chronically blocked. The barriers of ignorance, fear, and hostility severely hamper the organic functioning of the Holy City. Beyond the local pathologies, the conflict over Jerusalem/Al-Quds between Israelis and Palestinians threatens to explode into a regional conflagration with horrific suffering for everyone.

If we hold onto the image of Mother Jerusalem as a shared heart, both holy and diseased, a healing path to justice and peace may lead through her varied geography.

The ecumenical "Christian Quarter" resonates with the diversity of Christian life in Jerusalem over the centuries. I will leave it to Christians to decide whether this diversity is a positive sign of plurality within the Christian fold or whether the separate chapels within the Church of the Holy Sepulchre signify a tragic fragmentation, brokenness in the Body of Christ.

One Christian community has a quarter all its own: the Armenians. They were the first people to embrace Christianity as a national faith in the year 301, a decade before Constantine's rise to power. The Armenians are a deeply devout people, and their small Jerusalem community of about 1500 revolves around the ornate Cathedral of St. James. When one considers the distinctiveness of Armenian Christians and then juxtaposes their story with those of the Israelis and Palestinians in the adjacent Jewish and Muslim Quarters, a pattern with a significant message emerges.

These three peoples—the Armenians, Jews, and Palestinians—are rooted in the Holy Land for centuries through their respective traditions.

One common aspect of their religious heritages is a three-fold loyalty: to a people, to a faith tradition, and to a particular land. (For the Jews and Palestinians that land is the same, Israel/Palestine, while for the Armenians the holy homeland is Armenia).

On the level of the physical body, all three national communities have endured traumatic massacres: first the Armenian genocide at the hands of the Turks before and during World War I; then we Jews passed through the Valley of Death during World War II; and since then the Palestinians have suffered massacres perpetrated by virtually every other Middle Eastern people they have encountered. The Palestinian experience of displacement, dispossession, and occasional massacres can not be objectively compared with the genocide of the Armenians or of the Jews; yet a subjective sense of being survivor peoples, mourning their martyrs and affirming their communal dignity in the face of existential threat, does characterize all three national-religious communities.

The three peoples share yet another common denominator: all have suffered, in the 20th century, exile from their respective homelands. This is more an assault to the spirit than to the body. We Jews, of course, know what it means to be refugees, "strangers in a strange land," for close to 2500 years. Psalms 137 and 126 are ample testimony to the Jewish experience of exile and return. Now if, in this 21st century, we have been blessed to return once again to Jerusalem as a free people, and we rejoice over that homecoming as a central part of our destiny as Jews, while the Armenian and Palestinian peoples are suffering the pain of their own diasporas, there must be some lesson in this fateful intermingling of joy and sorrow, a lesson that is neither fatalistic nor deterministic, but, instead, points to a hopeful healing of our historic traumas.

One image that conveys the shared experience is of three abused and fearful individuals walking through darkness, holding flickering candles lit by their ancestors long ago to illuminate their way. Each of the three wanderers longs for the security of his lost homeland and for the chance to define himself again in positive terms after being defined negatively by others for so long. Each of them fears that, out of the darkness, some enemy will attack, making him a victim once again. None of the three is able to trust others who might help him overcome the trauma and the dread.

Then, suddenly, the three figures converge, and their candles illuminate each other's faces. Each experiences the shock of mutual recognition. In the human faces is a reflection of something mysteriously Divine, so that each can echo the wondrous exclamation of the wounded Jacob, renamed Israel upon uniting with his estranged brother Esau: "For I have truly seen Your face as though seeing the face of God." (Gen. 33:10).

An awareness of the Divine aspect of each other's identity would help us overcome our conditioned fears, loyalties, and animosities. The underlying, liberating truth is that the one Creator has made us all in the Divine Image, every person being infinitely precious and beloved in God's sight. Here on earth, our common forefather Abraham/Ibrahim and our mother city Jerusalem/Al-Quds make all of us sisters and brothers in the family of believers. If we could recognize one another in that spirit, even while dialoguing about distinct identities and vocations, we could work together to sanctify God's Holy Land and the entire creation, sharing the Divine blessing of Shalom."

THE OFFENSE OF LOVE

| Civil society is leading the church |

Scott Campbell (2010)

THE YEAR 1999 WAS A TIME OF FERMENT by gay marriage advocates in the United Methodist Church. Sixty-eight pastors in California co-celebrated a same gender union in January. None was ever disciplined. In March, the Rev. Greg Dell of Chicago was suspended for a year from his ministry for doing the same thing. Then, on November 17 the Rev. Jimmy Creech was convicted by a jury of 13 Nebraska United Methodist clergy of officiating at a same gender covenant service, a chargeable offense under the Discipline of the church. The penalty for his conviction was that his clergy orders, both as a deacon and an elder in the church, were permanently removed. He was given the ecclesiastical death penalty for the offense of love.

The hope of those who have enshrined the prohibition against this act of pastoral conscience in the language of "chargeable offenses" has been that intimidation would suppress the moral integrity of clergy who might otherwise be inclined to minister to the needs of gay and lesbian people in the same way they do to their heterosexual constituents. To some degree it has been a successful strategy. There have been no further trials or expulsions from the church over the last decade for this particular offense. That is not to say, of course, that there have not been pastors who have conducted same gender commitment services and, now, marriages in a number of places. The practice has simply been driven underground.

There have been a few exceptions to this retreat into secrecy. The Rev. Karen Oliveto, a San Francisco pastor, openly married a number of same gender couples after such marriages briefly became legal in that city. Charges were brought against her and subsequently resolved in meetings with her bishop. A group of retired clergy in New England, organized in 1999 and now numbering close to 100 members, pledged to make themselves available to perform such services. The group recently issued an open letter in which it acknowledged that many of its members have conducted such ceremonies and pledged that they will continue to do so. No charges have been filed to date.

Another exception is more recent. Thirteen clergy members affiliated with Dumbarton United Methodist Church in Washington DC, where same gender marriage recently became legal, have pledged to perform same- and opposite-gender marriages on the same basis. Their covenant reads in part:

"Today we affirm that God's grace is open to all, and we witness to that grace through our commitment to justice and equality in our congregation, the District of Columbia, the United Methodist Church, and the world. We will honor and celebrate the wedding of any couple, licensed in the District of Columbia, who seek to commit their lives to one another in marriage."

Not only did the pastors covenant with one another, but the church's board unanimously endorsed their intention. In a subsequent action the entire worshiping congregation of the church signed a document indicating their support for the decision taken by these clergy.

Dumbarton's action has initiated a flurry of conversation among other progressive pastors and congregations. Many are wondering whether the time has come to make public what has been taking place quietly for years. For some this is a question of strategy, while for others it is a matter of conscience. Bishop John Schol, leader of the Baltimore/Washington Area of The United Methodist Church, has informed all pastors that he will enforce the current Disciplinary prohibitions. His letter, while attempting to be pastoral in tone, was conspicuously deficient of any challenge to act prophetically for the sake of the Gospel. The clear implication was to raise again the specter of Jimmy Creech. The possibility of defrocking exists for each pastor who violates the rules.

So the question before the progressive movement (if indeed it is a movement and not simply an amalgamation of ideas) is whether this is a time to advance or retreat? Is it a time to hunker back down and quietly do in secret what we ought to be doing not only in the sight of God, but in the plain sight of the world? Or could this be a *kairos* moment in the life of this particular denomination and others as well? Could this be the time when clergy and other Christians might finally begin to find the courage of their convictions by refusing to give credibility to unjust laws within the church? Could it be a time for massive non-cooperation with those laws, a time when those called to serve as jurors in church trials would decide to mete out sentences that fit the crime? What should the penalty be for exercising (rather than exorcizing) pastoral conscience? How about a week away from pastoral duties to reflect on the "crime" of caring for all of God's people?

Jesus was crucified for the offense of love. Must the church continue to do the same thing in our own day?

I don't know whether this is such a moment, but I do know that there is something new in the air. Civil society is leading the church to look at itself. Courts and legislatures are extending civil rights to all citizens. Change is coming and those of us who believe the church can do better than it has are either going to have to make our witness or one day be ashamed that we did not.

One day our sons and daughters or our granddaughters and grandsons will look back on this time and wonder where we were in the fight. I further suspect that when they do, the name of Jimmy Creech will be remembered long after many who held onto their orders and retired without rocking the boat too much. I wonder: Can orders be restored posthumously?

THE STRANGE CASE
OF TIMOTHY McVEIGH

J. Philip Wogaman (2001)

HOW ARE WE TO THINK OF THE DEATH PENALTY in light of the case of Timothy McVeigh?

Even those who are opposed to capital punishment have to acknowledge that if anybody deserved to be executed, surely he does. In the deliberate, well-planned bombing of the Murrah Federal Building in Oklahoma City, he murdered 168 people, including 19 small children in the building's day care center. Even now, six years after this foul deed, he seems utterly remorseless—at least according to two reporters who interviewed him for 80 hours. Could a better illustration be offered in support of capital punishment?

Yet, what makes this such a strange case is his apparent eagerness to be executed. Referring to this as "state-assisted suicide," he refused to allow any further appeals in his behalf and insisted that the execution proceed. Now scheduled for May 16, this will be the first federal execution since 1963.

"State assisted suicide"? By executing him, are we giving him what he wants? And if that is the case, what does that do to the theory that the death penalty is a deterrent? In McVeigh's case, could it even be argued that the death penalty was not a deterrent but an incentive?!

That idea may seem strange. And yet, students of capital punishment have long concluded that it really does work in that perverse way—not in every case, to be sure, but often enough to give us pause.

The strangeness of this case is heightened by the clamor of many people to have the execution televised so they can see it.

You can almost understand the desire of some of those whose loved ones were killed by this man's deed to see him executed. Some, no doubt, believe it will bring a kind of closure to their spirits. I am skeptical that revenge brings such closure, but I do not stand in judgment of those who think it will. They are deserving of sympathy.

Still, there is a further irony. McVeigh himself evidently wants it to be televised. If it is to be televised for the benefit of a few hundred survivors, he will insist, he says, that it be televised for the whole country. I doubt he has the power to "insist" on anything, but again it raises questions about motive. Suppose he, or anybody else, does something terrible for the sake of personal publicity in an execution. Has the penalty again become an incentive and not a deterrent?

Some opponents of capital punishment advocate televising these gruesome executions in the thought that this would increase public abhorrence. I think that would be a terrible mistake. It could have exactly the opposite effect of brutalizing the popular culture, giving people perverse enjoyment of the spectacle of others dying. It happened in Rome!

Putting raw emotion aside as best we can, what stands out to me in the strange case of Timothy McVeigh is that murder expresses disrespect for life. That is obvious in the murderer's disregard for the lives of the victims. Less obvious, but no less true, is the murderer's disrespect for his or her own life. That seems true, on the face of it, in McVeigh's case. He's prepared to die—maybe even wants to die—because he doesn't want to live. Even murderers who kill for other motives, such as financial gain, seem to have a pretty low regard for the humanity in themselves as well as in others.

The country seems to be doing more soul-searching on this subject now. Maybe the churches can lead the way. At the United Methodist General Conference last May, the church's opposition to the death penalty was reaffirmed by a 97 percent margin. Surprising as that is, in light of public opinion in the United States, the action may indicate a new kind of attitude developing. In any case, the church's position reflects deeper spiritual insight than the passions that are aroused when the public is outraged.

EXPERIENCING TRAGEDY, DEEPENING COMPASSION
Scott Campbell (2005)

I AM SCHEDULED TO HELP LEAD A WORKSHOP for a group of English-speaking pastors in Hong Kong next February. The topic is one I would just as soon not be qualified to address. The working title is "Ministering through Personal Tragedy." The dual meaning of the title is intended, recognizing that pastors must continue to minister even when tragic events occur in their lives, and, also, that those very circumstances can become a powerful means of connecting with others.

I will be facilitating this workshop with David and Linda Marriott who serve the Hong Kong Union Church (David as pastor and Linda in numerous volunteer roles). They lost their 15 year-old son to suicide just over two years ago on the eve of his 16th birthday. As I have previously shared with readers of this column, my wife and I also lost a child last January when our 23 year-old daughter died of a drug overdose. David's invitation to participate in this event has caused me to reflect on what I might share with others.

I recognized immediately that I could not talk about "what I have learned" as if I have somehow made progress over this last year. The truth is, insight comes slowly in such circumstances. Advances are always accompanied by retreats. It is perhaps more appropriate to speak of discoveries.

The *first* and most important of these discoveries has been how blessed I have been to be in the church. From the first hours of our loss, our family was embraced by caring, loving people ministering to us in the name of Jesus Christ. We have received grace upon grace.

A few years ago, I asked a dear clergy friend who was only days from dying what he had learned in his encounter with death. The first thing he said was, "I have learned that everything I have preached about the power of grace is absolutely true." I understand now what he meant. It is one thing to describe to others a vision of the church. It is quite another to be sustained by the embodied grace of the community when you are not sure how you will take your next step.

A *second* discovery has been that it is important to tell the truth about your loss. Truth telling can take many forms. It does not mean that you indiscriminately recite intimate details to anyone who asks. But it does mean that you face what has happened in your life as forthrightly as you can, and, where appropriate, share your story.

This does at least two things. It frees you from the prison of pretence, allowing you to use your energy on what is real and not on maintaining façades. And it frees others more authentically to be themselves.

Not long ago I was talking with a young man who was coming to terms with some important questions about his own identity. One of the factors he cited as being important in his journey was the honesty with which people shared their prayer concerns at our church on Sunday mornings. "To hear someone raise a prayer concern for their nephew who is addicted to drugs was positively liberating" he said.

What I did not tell him was that the man who had offered that prayer concern had come to me a few weeks earlier and confided that he finally felt free to share his story with the congregation because my wife and I had been open about the cause of Suzanna's death. Honesty can be contagious. It is one of the characteristics that distinguish mere congregations from caring communities.

A *third* and much harder dynamic I have had to struggle with is recognizing that every situation I'm in is not about me. People go on living their lives quite independently of the grief that I may be carrying at any given moment. Their world hasn't stopped, and recognizing that to be so helps me to realize that my world also must continue.

Finally, related to the third point, I have discovered that I must recognize and accept that people aren't always going to say what I need to hear from them. I heard not long ago of a woman who attended her first meeting of Compassionate Friends, a self-help group for parents who have lost children. Her son had died of a heroin overdose, and she finally mustered the courage to go to a meeting. She was devastated as she listened to another parent grieving for her lost child who wondered, "Why did it have to be my son? Why couldn't it have been some drug addict?"

That woman could make a decision not to go back to Compassionate Friends, whether it was the right decision or not. A pastor does not have such a luxury. We are forced by the nature of what we do to focus on the needs of others. This does not mean that we cannot find ways to communicate our own needs to them, but we cannot simply react out of our hurt. I suspect this is not such a bad thing for any of us to learn.

In my experience, people do not say things with the intent of causing distress. It is often simply a matter of insensitivity or a misguided desire to be helpful. I find the Lord's Prayer to be tremendously useful in such situations. What a gift it is to have a daily reminder of our need to forgive and be forgiven! Forgiveness is a discipline, not an emotion.

The Dalai Lama spoke recently at Harvard. He told a story about a Buddhist monk who had been imprisoned by the Chinese for 20 years. Upon his release he came to visit the Dalai Lama.

"What was it like for you in prison?" his Holiness asked.

"There were several points along the way when I was in danger" replied the monk.

"What kind of danger?"

"I was in danger of losing my compassion for my Chinese captors."

Maybe the secret to ministering through personal tragedy, whether as a lay person or a member of the clergy, can be discovered at precisely that point—if we allow our own sorrows to deepen our compassion for others, we not only survive, we may even thrive.

CLASS STRUGGLE AND RELIGION

| Staying neutral isn't an option |

Joerg Rieger (2011)

UNTIL THE RECENT CONSERVATIVE ALLEGATIONS of class struggle that is being supposedly waged against the wealthy, this topic was even more difficult to bring up in polite company than politics, religion, sex, or money. Up to this point, talk about class struggle usually resulted in the accusation that those who dare to mention the term are the ones instigating it.

But the reality is different. Billionaire Warren Buffett has it right: There is class struggle, and the rich are winning it. A relatively small group keeps increasing its wealth and power at the expense of everyone else by participating in a sort of class struggle that is mostly invisible. Part of this struggle includes cuts in workers' pay and wage, major intensification of workload (speed-up), reneging on pension plans, reducing care, and increasing resistance to labor organizing itself.

This sort of class struggle is not named but justified by economic philosophies of trickle down and by quasi-religious beliefs that the free-market economy will benefit everybody in the long run and that a rising tide will lift all boats. In this context, workers and unions are often blamed for making unreasonable demands that jeopardize their companies despite evidence to the contrary. And here religion plays an essential role: the success of the class struggle that is waged from the top down depends on keeping the beliefs in the beneficial character of the market alive. No matter that these beliefs go in the face of reality, as the lack of a rising tide becomes the fate of more and more people and nothing of substance ever trickles down.

In this context, people of faith have some options: One option would be simply to ignore the clash between the classes, which is the default mode now and which explains the high level of discomfort when the notion of class struggle is even mentioned. Another option would be to declare this clash as real but part of another world that is irrelevant in the spheres of religion. Yet another option would be to use religion to heal whatever clash exists—a common response especially from mainline religious communities who quickly resort to notions of peace and harmony when confronted with tensions of any kind. None of these approaches, however, really captures the problem because none addresses the underlying power differentials.

The insights of liberation theologies, broadly conceived, are especially relevant at this point. Economist Michael Zweig, makes a significant observation about the difference of this approach to theology: "Liberation theology can be distinguished from liberal theology in that the former recognizes class conflict . . . and positions itself consciously as an ally of one class against the other; whereas liberal theology, which also seeks to ameliorate the conditions of capitalism and sees the need for structural changes, denies the class-conflictual nature of society and proposes instead a plan for social harmony among all the classes." While this may sound harsh and tendentious, similar conflicts and tensions are at the basis of the Judeo-Christian traditions from Moses to Jesus and Paul—all of whom took sides. Things tend to become clearer when conflict is realized rather than repressed.

Taking sides does not imply a lack of care about the other side: when Jesus took the sides of the people against the sides of the privileged of his own day, he cared about the salvation of both sides, knowing that true harmony can only be achieved if the tensions are addressed and overcome rather than repressed. His impassioned speeches against the Pharisees in Matthew 23, for instance, provide only one example for this: accusing them of having neglected "the weightier matters of the law: justice and mercy and faith" (Matthew 23:23) implies not so much an ultimate rejection but an invitation to conversion and a new beginning. Unfortunately, in both religion and economics, conflict is too often repressed and, thus, pushed out of sight, so it becomes even more harmful.

Dealing with the issue of class struggle, we need to ask ourselves what would change in religion and economics if we paid attention to those who are on the side that is loosing. Already the Apostle Paul, turning a classical imperial notion of society as a hierarchically ordered body on its head, understood that "if one member suffers, all suffer together with it" (1 Corinthians 12:26a). Pressure applied to the weakest tends to spread and will invariably destroy the body as a whole. Conversely, gains made in this context also spread: the unions have found that when wages are raised for some workers and when their working conditions improve, the wages and working conditions of all workers tend to improve. In Paul's language: "If one member is honored, all rejoice together with it" (1 Corinthians 12:26b). The Christian thing to do, in this context, is to take a stand with those who suffer and to work for change, which will ultimately benefit everyone.

poetry
Poetry
poetry
poetry
poetry

ONLY THROUGH YOUR LOVE WE CAN SURVIVE

| To the children who lost their parents on September 11, 2001 |

Ibrahim M. Abu-Rabi' (2008)

I fix my gaze on your eyes,
Trying the fathom the depth of your anguish
And the extent of your pain.

When your parents kissed you goodbye that morning
It never crossed your minds that you would never meet again;

Buried under the rubble, the bodies of your loved ones
Have dotted our emotional landscape
And have made you closer to our hearts than ever.

Your pain has thrown us into the unspoken pain of the millions
Of suffering children around the world, JUST like you;
The children of Afghanistan, Bosnia, Kosovo, Palestine, and Israel.

We feel as though our *raison d'etre*, foundation, and identity,
Has been shattered beyond belief
However, your beautiful and sad eyes give us
A glimmer of light, hope, and anchor;
We tread the path of agony, this time, not alone,
But in unison with you;
We surrender ourselves completely to you,
You have become our guide, just like the SAGE in Dante's *Divine Comedy*;
You have become our teachers, giving us lessons in love,
Humility, and compassion;
We see on the horizons the beginnings of a new dawn;
We see your compassionate smile
Taking us by the hand in the new darkness
Surrounding the world.
Your proximity to us has made life meaningful again.

Yes, we will overcome this tragedy together;
Yes, we will overcome it together with the suffering children of the world
When? We do not know!
The world seems to be poised on creating
More suffering for children like you
But We are sure that one day we will overcome;
We are sure that one day your smile will melt down all the anger
And hatred of this world.

'MOCRACY

Brian Wren (2003)

'Mocracy
dear friends we bring
in helicopter
gunships
it is our burden and our destiny
to give you
'Mocracy
elections votes campaigns
and credit-worthy leaders pre-approved
to give us forward bases handshakes smiles
and revenue
to prime the pump
for future wars
to globalize our manifest desire
for free compliant friendly
'Mocracy.

IN THE TIME OF THE TUMULT OF NATIONS
Samuel Hazo (2005)

We thought that the worst was behind us
in the time of the tumult of nations.
We planned and we saved for the future
in the time of the tumult of nations.
The crowds in the streets were uneasy
in the time of the tumult of nations.
We murdered our annual victims
in the time of the tumult of nations.
We were fined if we smoked in the cities
in the time of the tumult of nations.
We gave and deducted our givings
in the time of the tumult of nations.
We kept the bad news from the children
in the time of the tumult of nations.
We wakened from nightmares with headaches
in the time of the tumult of nations.

We voted for men we distrusted
in the time, in the time, in the time,
in the time of the tumult of nations.

In the time of the tumult of nations
the ones who were wrong were the loudest.
In the time of the tumult of nations
the poets were thought to be crazy.
In the time of the tumult of nations
the President answered no questions.
In the time of the tumult of nations
protesters were treated like traitors.
In the time of the tumult of nations
the airports were guarded by soldiers.
In the time of the tumult of nations
young women kept mace in their purses.
In the time of the tumult of nations
the rich were exempt in their mansions.
In the time of the tumult of nations
we waited for trouble to happen.
In the time of the tumult of nations
we lived for the weekends like children.

Like children we clung to our playthings
in the time of the tumult of nations.
We huddled in burglar-proof houses
in the time of the tumult of nations.
We said that the poor had it coming
in the time of the tumult of nations.
We readied our hand guns for trouble
in the time of the tumult of nations.
We tuned in to war every evening
in the time of the tumult of nations.
We watched as the bombs burned the cities
in the time of the tumult of nations.

The name of the game was destruction
in the time of the tumult of nations.
We knew we were once better people
in the time of the tumult of nations.
We pretend we are still the same people
in the time, in the time, in the time,
in the time of the tumult of nations.

YOUR BREATH UPON ME

| With appreciation to David and the 23rd Psalm |

Lyman Randall (2003)

Lord, you embrace me always.
You kiss my eyelids awake each morning and asleep each night.
You nurture my soul.
You light my path so I can follow you.

When I am lost, you give me courage.
When I feel abandoned, you touch my heart.
When I am sick, you heal my afflictions.
Your presence comforts me.

My life becomes more because of you.
You call forth abundance in the midst of scarcity.
Beauty and goodness surround me through your grace.
And my heart fills with hope as I pray
For your breath upon me forevermore.

TOUR SEVEN
Mary Kennan Herbert (2007)

We bought a small tract house,
suburban box like the one my parents had.
Sunlight slanted through the windows.
It was new, it was all the same.
Sure enough, Mr. Death showed up
to mow the lawn, to barbecue.
The story is new and then not.
It becomes tiresome and banal.
Yet each house has a different story.
The walls talk, spill their guts.
I still look out windows.
The slant of sunlight is the same.
not as much fun as opening it.
Mostly I remember the proud
new owner posing in front,
spreading arms wide to show
possession, or maybe joy, now lost.

Homeowner, you reminded me
of the crucifix above the bedroom door.
Pinned like a dead butterfly,
we reach the edge of property,
the limits of gardens and dreams.
We settle for a flattened planet,
prayer by rote. When can we soar?
What became of the guy on the cross?

DOING THE TRUTH
Richard M. Gray (2008)

"Moral values" seem to be the watchwords of the day,
And surely those who say they're not important must be few;
But in the end, it matters very little what we say,
What matters, and it matters greatly, lies in what we do.
The prophet Micah said it well, for those with ears to hear:
"What does the Lord require of those whose feet this earth would trod,
But to do justice, love kindness, and with hearts sincere,
To walk gently, humbly, with a just and loving God."
How can we, then, pursue a war whose cause was less than clear?
Or borrow sums of money we know we cannot pay,
To ease the burden on the few who have no cause to fear
And pass it on to generations of some future day?
How can we legislate the choices women need to make,
Or foreclose the chance to cure insufferable disease?
Deny to some the health in which we all have a stake,
Or tell the children left behind there are no remedies?
If truth itself resides entirely in the things we do,

Our doing must reflect somehow the things we're mindful of.
This match remains the measure of an axiom that's true:
The only moral value of significance is love.

REFLECTION
ReflectioN
refLECTion
REFLECTion
reflection
Reflection
reflECTION

THE OFFERING

| 1 John 4:7-12; Numbers 18:21-29 |

Anne Robertson (2003)

YOU'VE HEARD IT SAID THAT a person "knows just enough to be dangerous." That doesn't necessarily mean a person is learning to be violent. It just means that when we know a little bit about something, we might act in a way that we would never do if we knew more. This was clearly the case for me before I went into ministry and was working as a lay person in a church in Florida.

My issue was with the offering. I had no issue with taking up the offering or with giving. My family trained me to give ten percent of my income when I was a teenager, and I have always kept that up, gladly. My issue was with the practice of putting the offering plates on the altar after the plates were full. The little bit of knowledge I had told me that the altar was where important things went, and it seemed to me that we were glorifying money when we put the plates on the altar.

That thought grew and grew in my mind until I could hardly stand it.

We were worshiping money, I thought. It's not right! So I began to complain, loudly. I got others on my side, and I'm sure the pastor must have prayed nightly for something to happen to me in my sleep. Finally, I voiced my complaint to one woman in the church who simply said, "Oh, I just always assumed that since the altar was the place of sacrifice, that's where the money we sacrifice to God should go." Bingo. The light shone, and the pastor rested well from that point onward.

I had a little bit of information: The altar was where important things go. But, I didn't have the greater information about the altar as a place of sacrifice, a place of offering; and that other information made all the difference. Now I'm the one who puts the plates on the altar, and I really like doing it. I like lifting them up to God as our offering.

Remembering the struggle I had and knowing the struggles we all have around issues of money, I decided to do some teaching on what the offering is and does. Its roots go way back in the Old Testament to when Israel was formed as a nation. There were 12 different tribes that made up the nation of Israel. Actually, the whole nation was related since the 12 tribes were the descendants of the 12 sons of one man.

When the 12 tribes came into the land of Canaan, what is now Palestine, 11 of the 12 tribes were given land to settle. The twelfth tribe, the tribe of Levi, was not given any land. It was given a job instead. God told Moses that the tribe of Levi was to spend all its time and energy taking care of the tabernacle, which was the moveable tent that later became the temple. In Christian language, the tribe of Levi was told that it was to work full time in the church.

Because of that, the Levites would have no time left over to grow crops or herd animals and would therefore have no food and no way to provide for their families. But church workers deserved their wages just as much as others, so God came up with the idea of the tithe. God said to the other 11 tribes, "Okay, the Levites are performing an important service. They are making sure that the worship of God stays active and true in the community. Since that takes all their time, the rest of you need to bring ten percent of everything you get to them so they can provide for themselves and for their families." That's what a tithe is, giving ten percent for the support and maintenance of the church and its workers.

And no cheating, says God. Don't bring the leftover sour stuff for the Levites. Farmers, bring ten percent of your best crops. Shepherds, don't go bringing diseased animals; bring the good ones, the best ones. And so the practice of the tithe began. People brought tithes, and they also brought offerings, which were additional gifts above and beyond the tithe to help the poor and needy. That is why each Sunday when I ask the ushers to come forward, I instruct them to bring their tithes and offerings. They are distinct things. Tithes support the maintenance of the church, and the offerings are given to those in need.

That was still the system in Jesus' day, and after Jesus' death and resurrection, the early church gave it still more meaning. In the early days of the church, after Jewish Christians had been booted from the synagogues and before the church was established as an institution, there wasn't really anything like the temple to be maintained. "The church" was simply gatherings of people in different homes where they studied together, told the good news about Jesus, and shared in a meal together, which they brought potluck.

They didn't really need a tithe to support a building or workers anymore, but they did still need offerings. They needed to care for the poor and the widows and orphans. We see in the book of Acts that Paul traveled to the churches in Asia Minor and asked them to contribute to an offering for the poor back in Jerusalem.

This is a gross oversimplification, but hundreds of years went by, and finally the Roman Emperor Constantine decided that Christianity should be the official religion of the Empire. Freed from persecution and officially supported by the state, churches could really put down roots: build cathedrals, support schools for religious training, and all sorts of things. Voila! Now there is again a need for maintenance. There is still a need to give to the charitable work of the church, however, so the need for the tithe returns and the need for the offerings remains.

Up until the last few hundred years, however, the "offering" time in the worship service was completely tied to the sacrament of communion. As Cyril Richardson describes in his book *The Church Throughout The Centuries*:

"Each Christian brought some bread and wine and this was collected by the deacons and consecrated by the bishop or elders, so that the united offerings of the people became one sacrament. At the Eucharist they also gave freely of their substance (in kind as well as in money) for the aid of the shipwrecked sailors, orphans, widows, captives, and unemployed. All Christians in need were cared for and nourished from this liberal treasury. Their corporate devotion and their practical life of love were knit together in real unity."

What that meant is that, during a worship service, the offering of the people was a direct response to the offering of Christ for us. The passage we read from I John says that we love because God first loved us. That is why we give as well. We give because God first gave to us.

When the offering is a response to what God has already given to us, then we are in a better position to understand the practices of some cultures where the offering is the highlight of the worship service. I share Thanksgiving dinner each year with a Christian man from Ghana. We got to talking about the offering one year, and he told me about how much fun that is in his church in Ghana. People don't wait for the plates to be passed to them. They literally get up and dance their way to the front, eager to bring any gift they can to the God who has given them life. That portion of the service has been known to last an hour. He said he missed that here. He said that churches here didn't seem to enjoy the offering, and he was completely baffled by our lack of enthusiasm.

In a number of churches today the connection between God's self-giving and our giving is kept by having the communion elements brought forward when the plates are brought forward, so that we can remember that when God gives, God gives everything: broken body, shed blood. God is a generous, abundant giver, and it is that giving that we are called to emulate as we try to become more like Jesus when we say we are disciples. Disciples do what the teacher does, and in this case the teacher, Jesus, gives.

So that is what the offering time is all about. If the church wants to go back to the way it was very early on, we wouldn't need the tithes. If you want to get rid of the buildings and trained teachers, you can just gather in homes each week, share your faith with each other and bring a covered dish for dinner. As you sit around that fuller table of communion and recall what Jesus gave to us, your own giving to those in need should be a mirror of and a response to Christ's gift to you.

But, if you want to gather together in larger numbers in a comfortable space, if you want to be inspired by excellent music, want programs for yourselves and for your children, and want to have the benefit of trained leadership, then God's provision in the Hebrew Scriptures is again appropriate. We need the tithes as well as the offerings. The amazing thing to me is that across four thousand years, inflation has not touched the church's need. Ten percent would still do it. If everybody just took for granted that ten percent of income goes for the work of the church, we would never see another financial campaign, never have to sign another pledge card. Our needs would be met, and we could focus on the real work of the Body of Christ.

During our worship service, we put the offering after the sermon to show that our offering of money is a response to the Word of God. It is a response to the Good News proclaimed to us that God loves us so much that God would go so far as to become human, to live and die as one of us in order to win our love. We love because God first loved us. We give because God first gave to us. We give because God took the sting out of death for us. We give because that's what lovers do.

I am so grateful that my parents taught me to tithe and to give, not just because it is a good discipline that helps me keep money in its proper place in my life, but because it's fun. Even before my giving was helping to pay my own salary, I loved the feeling of giving, both to the church and to individuals in need. One of my dreams has been to one day have enough money to go into a shabby restaurant in a poor area and tip the waitress a thousand dollars, just because it would be fun. I would love to march over to the Humane Society and plunk a million dollars down on somebody's desk and say, "Here, build a new facility."

I don't like to be put on a guilt trip about giving. Nobody does. What I'm trying to say is that, just like my experience with the offering plates on the altar, there comes a point in Christian life when the light bulb goes on, when what was once an objection is fully understood and integrated, and it becomes a joy. There was a point in my life of giving that I gave because it was my duty. God said to do it, so I did. But I grew from that point, and now it is a joy, a joyful response to the God who first loved and gave to me.

And you?

A FRIEND GOES TO IRAQ TO WITNESS FOR PEACE
Cynthia B. Astle (2003)

SELDOM HAVE I KNOWN SUCH COURAGE as the courage of Weldon Nisly.

In the waning hours of President Bush's ultimatum to Saddam Hussein, Weldon and a Christian Peacemaker Team left for Iraq. Their mission was to serve as witnesses to the impact of U.S. military action from within the country.

Surprised by Weldon's news, I wept as I sent my friend a last-minute e-mail of my prayers and support. I was terrified for his welfare, and that of his team, the Iraqi people and the American military. I was terrified because Weldon went into the desert, as Jesus went into the desert, to face our wild beasts of temptation—our unrestrained power, our national arrogance, our fear of death.

As it turned out, my fears were justified. The car carrying Weldon's team out of Iraq, traveling at 80 mph to avoid U.S. and British bombs, blew a tire on the road from Baghdad to Amman, Jordan. Their car rolled down a 10-foot embankment and all the occupants were injured. Weldon suffered multiple rib fractures and a broken thumb.

Remarkably, all were treated for free at the last remaining medical clinic in nearby Rutba, Iraq, where an English-speaking doctor told them "we are all part of the same human family."

In the midst of my terror then and my sadness now I have rejoiced, because I know that Weldon has sacrificed his comfortable life as pastor of Seattle Mennonite Church to stand up for Jesus's 'third way' outlined in the Gospel. He, his family and his church went through deep, prayerful discernment about God's call for him to wage peace. Their process has been hard and painful, yet they sent him freely, in obedience to Jesus' teaching in Mark 8:31-38.

In his message to his friends among the Network of Biblical Storytellers, where Weldon and I met, he included his first two Lenten sermons. Here in his own words is part of his rationale for his bold act:

"It is not that war is too strong a response to the evils of Saddam Hussein, it is that war is too weak a response. It is weak because it is a response of fear and force that leaves in its wake more suffering, more disparity, more anger, all leading to more terrorism. It is not hard to guess where future targets of terrorism will be directed.

"Whether or not bombing the hell out of Iraq ever destroys Saddam Hussein, we can expect that in its wake will come waves of more hatred and more terrorism and more fear and more insecurity and more madness."

By the world's standards, Weldon's trip to Iraq was misguided, foolish, even unpatriotic. By the standard of our faith as expressed in Scripture, he did exactly what Christ would have him do, despite the ridicule and danger associated with his act.

To me this radical sacrifice of Christian dissent to "the powers that be," as Walter Wink terms it, makes Weldon and his companions prophets for our tragic time. They put themselves in harm's way in hopes we will see that our collective danger comes not from lack of security, but from the consequences of our greed and power.

I am proud that Weldon is my friend and brother in Christ. I pray that we who profess to follow Christ will be inspired by his courage to stand up for the Gospel when our time comes.

PREACHING TO THE EASTER-ONLY CROWD
Donna Schaper (2004)

THERE IS ONE BIG PROHIBITION and a half-dozen permissions when it comes to preaching to the *Easter*-only crowd. The prohibition is obvious. Make no reference whatsoever to the fact that you haven't seen much of them lately.

That is like yelling at a teenager who has just cleaned up his room by saying, sarcastically, "It's about time."

Reward the positive behavior; do not punish the past. Punishment only works when we catch people in the act: that means we can call them some Sundays at 10 a.m. and get somewhere with negative remarks.

When a family or person has come back, it is prodigal time. It is welcome time. It is a time for feast and great joy.

Toe-dippers in Christianity deserve the same respect as the fully immersed. Jesus may even prefer some of these skeptics to those of us who have become self-righteously convinced. As Bishop Spong so rightly says, the "Church-Alumni Association" is the fastest growing religious organization in America, even more in numbers than the evangelicals and fundamentalists. If we want to reverse that trend, welcome is advised when strangers shadow and "darken" our doors.

Manners are everything on EASTER and other big crowd days. More positively, what we can do is to make sure the service is as transparent as possible. It should be simple and short.

The bulletin needs to be readable by someone in the sixth grade. It needs to make sense. There need to be no ``little'' mistakes like forgetting the ``to stand'' asterisk on the last hymn so the newcomer doesn't know to stand, even though the regulars do. There need to be no confusions about standing or sitting whatsoever. There need to be no bulletin bloopers that cause an ``irregular'' to feel more uncomfortable than he or she already feels.

Think about the irregular as feeling like they are wearing a big sign that says, ``I'm new.'' Think from their side of the pew, as the service is prepared. If there is a sharing of the peace or physical time in the service when people greet each other with the kiss or handshake of peace, make sure it is fully explained before it happens.

Also, today is not the time for the preacher to tell everything he or she knows about the Resurrection. Simple is better. Short is best. People who aren't coming to church regularly probably have been bruised by church somehow. Either people or preachers have insulted them. We need to take very few risks in repeating whatever behavior originally offended.

If regular Christians are getting nervous about your manners by now, good. You might want to take a look at a painting as a form of spiritual preparation for the service. I recommend Marc Chagall's painting called Crucifixion. There we see a jumbo crowd beneath the cross of Jesus. There we find a quiet and meditative way to prepare ourselves spiritually as well as practically for our guests.

Gaze at (Russian Hasidic Jewish) Chagall's crowd and be reminded once again that salvation is ``what all flesh shall see together.''

Look at that crowd - almost as if the artist knew one day that the 6-billionth baby would be born. Look at that crowd with the artist's simultaneity: This is an eternal, not a timed moment.

Or think of EASTER and its guests as boarding a jumbo jet. A child speaking three languages will sit ahead of us in claustrophobic community. Gays will sit next to straights on the jumbo jet. The Jesus of love will make room for them all, in a way not even the best preacher can actually imagine. A family of five from will occupy the middle seat, all playing cards and giggling. The boys will be poking each other.

Some of the guests will have just discovered that they have cancer. Others will have been beaten by their spouse the night before. Still others will have discovered marijuana in their children's sneakers.

We ride this jet, we enter this holy service of the Easter festival all together beneath the cross of Jesus, clutter clutched to our hearts, self-preservation continuing its old drum beat - in the air, on the ground, wherever. Those who are in will try to keep those who are out, out, but fortunately we will fail because of the size of our salvation.

The cross makes us new. How? In how we address the person in the seat next to us. The new will come in new relationships, just as Jesus warned eternally, saying that he lived and died so that we might love one another.

The new will be in relationships to what we don't know but do want to know about each other. The new will be in little packages, packed tightly beneath the cross of Jesus, in urgent expectation.

WE WOULD HAVE TRUSTED HIM WITH THE WORLD
Jennifer Latham (2003)

PICTURE THIS: A THIRTEEN-YEAR-OLD, chubby but very sincere girl starts off her oral biography presentation in eighth grade English class by walking to the front of the room singing, "It's a Beautiful Day in the Neighborhood," changing from dress shoes into Keds, and trading a jacket for a cardigan. Now, if you now even the tiniest bit about eighth graders, you probably have an idea about how this display was received. Yes, this really happened, and yes, I was the girl. And you know what? I wouldn't change having done this as my introduction for Mr. Rogers' biography for the world because he would have been proud of me.

As you likely know, Mr. Rogers died after a short battle with stomach cancer this February, leaving a palpable gap not only in the world of children's television, but in the fabric of American culture as well. There is much to be said about his life, and you could fill pages with biographical facts and discussions of the more than two hundred awards and honorary degrees he received. But this kind of information is not what matters most about the life of this gentle and unfailingly kind man any more than the rather basic appearance of the sets and puppets on *Mr. Rogers' Neighborhood* are what mattered about the show.

In a radio interview with NPR's Diane Rehm a few years back, Mr. Rogers described how he knew he wanted to work in television from the moment he first watched it during a college break. From the start he recognized the tremendous power behind a device that would allow him basically to enter into families' homes and speak with them. So, after graduating from Rollins College in 1951 with a degree in music composition, he began working in production at NBC. By 1953 he had already found a way out of commercial television and into the new arena of children's programming.

The roots of *Mr. Rogers' Neighborhood* emerged at WQED Pittsburgh, where he worked with host Josey Carey to produce *The Children's Corner*. Although only his voice and puppeteering skills were featured on the show, it was largely defined by Mr. Rogers' developmentally-focused technique of using straightforward, on-screen discussions to address issues of concern to children. Based on his Master's studies at the University of Pittsburgh's Graduate School of Child Development, this approach was to become not only his trademark, but the cornerstone of the Presbyterian ministry he trained for Pitt as well.

After working briefly for the Canadian Broadcasting Corporation on a show called *Misterogers*, he returned to WQED in Pittsburgh and began work on the early episodes of *Mister Rogers' Neigborhood*. Thirty-three years later in 2001, he and his veteran crew had created over 900 episodes. Amazingly, Mr. Rogers was the executive producer for each episode, wrote every single script, and penned over 200 songs (most of which were used on the shows) in his lifetime.

But none of this information explains his magic. What about Mr. Rogers made Gloria Steinem say that he was, "The only human being on TV to whom you would entrust the future of the world?" I'm pretty sure that for Ms. Steinem it wasn't the fact that he was an ordained minister. Mr. Rogers never made a big deal about that, although he certainly didn't keep it a secret. Maybe it was the way he earned our trust by always talking to us directly and warmly about things that mattered. Or that he never propped himself up on degrees or titles, never assumed a position of moral superiority.

Rather than teach his valuable lessons in terms of a god who was not universal to all of his viewers and their families (let alone relevant to young children with limited capacities for dealing with complex and inherently abstract notions of religion), Mr. Rogers relied on the strength of example. Through secular words, stories, and songs, he made a difference in more young lives than he could have ever hoped to reach from a pulpit. Instead of doctrine or dogma, Mr. Rogers taught the fundamental values he believed were central to his religious calling: kindness, caring, generosity, honesty, public service, love, and recognizing the dignity and value in every human being.

ONE OF THE MOST UNIQUE THINGS about *Mister Rogers' Neighborhood* was its focus on social and emotional development. While other children's shows based their content on cognitive development (letters, numbers, phonics, and such), Mr. Rogers focused almost entirely on things like what to do when you get angry, or how it's normal to be sad when your goldfish dies. He taught more than one generation that the things they feel inside are important, and reassured us that no feelings are bad. At the same time, he told us that some ways of dealing with feelings are OK, while others are not.

Mr. Rogers also made a calculated decision never to appear in the Neighborhood of Make Believe-land, where favorite characters like Lady Elaine Fairchilde and Daniel Striped Tiger lived. With a short trolley trip, children could share in a fantasy world filled with puppet characters who worked through all sorts of issues with the help of caring adults other than Mr. Rogers. By placing those adults in Make Believe-land, the show reassured children that imagination and fantasy are not only normal, but that adults rely on them too. And with the equally short trolley trip back into Mr. Rogers' living room, children were reassured that our internal fantasy worlds are only a part of our lives as a whole.

Another of Mr. Rogers' greatest gifts was his ability to recognize the potential in new technologies. From day one he saw that television could be used for more pure entertainment. And as computers and video game technology evolved, he never condemned children's involvement with them. In one interview, he was quick to reassure a fellow grandfather that while some video games are not appropriate for children, many are not only entertaining, but educational as well.

In that same interview, a mother called in to describe how she and her children, including a son diagnosed with autism, watched *Mr. Rogers Neighborhood* together years ago. Despite his general lack of interest in his external world, she said that her autistic son would, without fail, turn to watch the television when the show came on. She credited Mr. Rogers with being largely responsible for helping her son establish a foundation for interacting with the world around him, and went on to say that her son is now married and has a child. As you can imagine, Mr. Rogers' voice was choked with tears when he responded to her. But it was his actual response that conveyed his gift for making children and adults alike feel good about themselves. He thanked her for giving him one of the greatest gifts he could hope for, and then immediately pointed out what remarkable parents she and her husband were for giving their son the time and the room he needed to develop at his own pace.

Such was Mr. Rogers's selflessness and caring for other people that he could unfailingly turn any discussion into an enriching experience for the other person. In this way he not only helped children feel secure about their worlds, but exuded a calming air of parental confidence that gave adults a model from which to base their own parenting strategies.

Mr. Rogers once said, "I think we're created deep and simple, and society doesn't nurture that. Society nurtures shallow and complicated." This simple philosophical observation guided not only his program, but his life as well. So far as I could find, there is not a single indication from friends, co-workers, or even cynical reporters that Mr. Rogers was anything other than the man we saw on his show. And judging from the media response to the news of his death, Americans share a true sense of having lost our TV father. Oh, and as for the reaction of my eighth grade classmates to my presentation; well, you'd be surprised. I wasn't teased or made to feel silly by a single one of them. It seems that something in Mr. Rogers' message was strong enough to withstand even the social pressure cooker of eighth grade.

Mr. Rogers, you will be missed.

CREATING A FUTURE WORTHY OF OUR PAST

Lovett H. Weems, Jr. (2000)

WHAT WORDS WILL BEST DESCRIBE United Methodism in the 21st Century?

Some words to describe United Methodism in the United States in past centuries might be:
- 18th Century - Fervor and Marginality
- 19th Century - Growth and Establishment
- 20th Century - Mature and Declining

But what about the 21st Century?

Denominations, as all organizations, experience life cycles not unlike human beings. For most of the last century, United Methodism in the United States has been a very "mature" organization, well established but in decline. Great strength comes with maturity. Yet there are particular pitfalls for mature organizations not faced in the same way by emerging movements.

Organizational Temptation: Competing Values Supercede Mission
Redemptive Opportunity: All Serve a Common Mission

Mature organizations tend to confuse mission and values. Mission is what we exist to do. Values are the commitments we honor as we do our work to accomplish the mission. Both mission and values are important and essential, but mission is the guide. Values do not compete with mission, but rather shape how the mission is fulfilled.

In mature organizations, people may begin choosing the values they like most and defending them against competing values. They tend to forget the mission they are called to serve. Today in our church many values compete for attention-evangelism, ecumenism, inclusiveness, diversity, justice, spirituality, and so on. As people cling desperately to the values they most appreciate, instead of joining to serve a common mission, the organization becomes fractured and continues to decline. Decline only causes people to become more uneasy, so they cling more tightly to what they most fear losing. Division and decline continue.

Organizational Temptation: Turn Inward
Redemptive Opportunity: Focus Outward

Mature organizations tend to lose their outward missional stance and increasingly turn their primary attention inward. Peter Drucker says thriving organizations practice "outside to inside" thinking rather than the more common "inside to outside" thinking. The key difference is the starting point. Do we start with our needs, values, and goals, or with the needs, hopes, and dreams of those we exist to serve? In "outside to inside" thinking, one always responds out of one's mission and values, but the external starting point makes all the difference.

Unfortunately, many serving institutions, including the church, tend to be dominated by people who feel they know what people need better than the people they exist to serve know. Ordinary church members and especially those not in the church, are rarely asked.

A pastor had completed one year of service. The first year had been filled with conflict over differing assumptions about appropriate worship. The good thing was that the pastor recognized that some assumptions had been imposed that were not culturally fitting. The bad news was that, while the pastor knew what to stop doing, there was no clue as to what might be substituted. Seeking counsel from a former teacher, the pastor was advised, "Just ask them," to which the pastor replied, "I have. I have asked many pastors what I should do."

It had never occurred to this pastor to ask the people some simple questions such as "What is it about worship that means the most to you?" The pastor as worship leader will still respond to suggestions with theological, historical, and pastoral integrity. Only now the pastor has the knowledge needed to lead in a way that honors the values and meets the needs of both congregation and pastor.

Organizational Temptation: Power Is Seen as a Limited and Scarce Commodity
Redemptive Opportunity: Power Becomes a Limitless and Plentiful Resource

There is a fixation in many mature organizations on power for oneself, and a suspicion of power for others.

This fixation on power and influence causes groups to seek more power for themselves by taking it away from others, as if power were a fixed sum like a pie, i.e., the larger the piece you get, the smaller piece I must get. So one group tries to have more power by taking it from another. Instead, we should be seeing how we can make each other stronger for our own special callings. The key question becomes not how much power each group has, but what is the calling each of us has.

What might it mean to find lay people saying "How do we make our clergy stronger for their callings?" and clergy saying "How do we make laity stronger for their callings?" You would find the senior pastor asking how the youth pastor can be strengthened as the leader for this area of ministry. And the youth minister would be asking how the senior pastor might be made stronger for the calling that goes with that office. You would find large membership churches saying "How do we make sure that small membership churches are strengthened in order to fulfill the mission that only they can do?" And you would find small membership churches saying "How do we make sure that large membership churches are strengthened so they can fulfill the their unique calling?"

When we do this, we will discover that power, instead of being a fixed sum, is an expandable pie. The more you have, the more I have.

The more I am willing to be influenced by you, the more willing you are to be influenced by me. There is more power for everyone. And the church grows in strength.

> *Organizational Temptation: Prerogatives Are Protected*
> *Redemptive Opportunity: New Missional Frontiers Are Pursued*

People in mature and declining organizations become anxious. They may think, "There may not be as much as there used to be, but I want to make sure there is still a place for me." There is more concern about one's place in the organization than concern for the decline of the organization. There is more concern for rights and prerogatives and less interest in what new frontiers of mission God is presenting. Some leaders would rather have inordinate control in a smaller, deteriorating organization than to have a more appropriate role with many others in a thriving organization clearly focused on its mission.

One of the saddest tendencies in mature and declining organizations is for people to seek power in the organization and the satisfaction that power brings as a substitute for the witness and influence the organization has lost. Therefore, you have lay people seeking inordinate control within a local church as a substitute for the influence that the local church has lost in its community. You find clergy and laity seeking inordinate influence and control within their judicatories as a substitute for the influence that the church has lost within its culture. And you find people seeking control within a denomination because they have lost confidence that we are truly reforming the nation and spreading scriptural holiness across the land.

Conclusion

In the early days of a movement, there is a focused mission and clear vision. There is a fit between mission and needs, or the new venture will not succeed. In this time of intense passion, virtually all energy is focused on the vision. Such intense commitment establishes strength and growth.

The most dangerous time for an organization is a time of success. Greater complexity and attention are required by the additional forms, structures, and facilities now required for the newly established organization to continue and grow. Eventually, a gap between the original vision and the current organization will develop and, without revisioning, the organization will struggle to maintain the success it has achieved. Indeed, decline often follows maturity.

The question facing us as contemporary heirs of a rich heritage is, "Can we create a future worthy of our past?" Without a new vision, the future does not look bright. If United Methodist membership decline continues, for example, then in the first decade of the 21st century membership as a percentage of population will drop to the same level as it was in the first decade of the 19th century.

It does not have to be that way. Indeed, it is in times of hardship that new visions often emerge. It was in a time of despair that Nehemiah and his people united to rebuild the wall. It was after hundreds of years of suffering that Habakkuk sought and received the vision that the just shall live by faith. In was in the midst of life-denying realities that Jesus proclaimed that all might have abundant life.

Would it not be wonderful if at some future General Conference a speaker addressing the conference might make the following statement and immediately all heads nod in instant recognition of its truth:

As I think back on United Methodism in recent times, the only fitting description is in the words written years ago to the church at Thyatira. "I know all your ways, your love and faithfulness, your good service and your fortitude; and of late you have done even better than at first" (Rev. 2:19 NEB).

NEW CONSCIOUSNESS

| The emergent church and the world as sacrament |

Thomas Ambrogi (2010)

THE EMERGING CHURCH is the center of attention in much current theological thinking and discussion. Sometimes it's called the emergent church, depending on how much definitive clarity one claims to have about what is certainly happening. In any case, more and more people declare themselves to be spiritual, but not religious, find the institutional church irrelevant to their search, and prefer to divorce themselves from institutional structures.

So where is church, or what is church, for people on this mysterious edge of disturbing new consciousness? Or, even more fundamentally, who is God, or where is God to be found, or who is Christ, and where is Christ to be found in all this?

I resonate profoundly to the theological depth of these questions. I am a married Catholic priest, and my journey has included being a Jesuit theology professor in seminary and university, an ecumenical theologian, and a political and social activist in the broad religious community for some four decades now.

There is a new birthing happening in Western spirituality, and many see it is every bit as revolutionary as the 95 Theses which Martin Luther nailed to the Wittenberg door in 1517. Vast and dispersed, the new reformation is discovering the God of Becoming. And in undertaking this, the Church at work is not a denomination or an institution, there are no official leaders, and there is no serious level of organization. If we ask seriously where both church and God are to be found in the "emerging" revolution, it is possible to find some theological clues in a rebirth of both Incarnation and the spiritual richness of Sacramentality.

In an article called "The Breath of Life: Christian Ecology Begins With Incarnation," theologian John Garvey says: "The Incarnation is what makes Christian monotheism unique, and radically different from both Judaism and Islam. While the holiness of creation is certainly central to both these other traditions, the idea that what is essentially animal and mortal can be inhabited and transformed by God, that flesh itself can be transcendently holy, a created place where the uncreated resides, like the burning bush—this idea is central only to Christianity." This is an insight that needs to be savored carefully. Christian Ecology, he says, ought to celebrate its own theological roots in Incarnation, and be driven deeply by that vision.

Creation itself is God's great self-communication. The created world points beyond itself to the creator. And this is why the Jesuit paleontologist and visionary, Pierre Teilhard de Chardin, has been one of my greatest gurus. He insists with passionate beauty that human experience, far from being untrustworthy or contemptible, is God's way of being in the world, that all of creation is sacrament, is precisely The Divine Milieu.

So where is emerging church to be found today? It is found wherever the believing community gathers to support one another in pursuing the transformation of the world, consciously celebrating and trusting in the recreating power of the Spirit within that world.

For its very life, that community must come together to share the Gospel Word as the Good News. This can well happen in ritual and worship (even a potluck supper now and then!) in the steepled church on the street-corner, or in any other inviting community space such as a family living room around the fire. What is important is that there be at least a few risk-takers and theological adventurers, and that the gathering be, before all else, Spirit-led organizing to bring peace to a war-torn world, health care for all, justice in the sweatshop and in the union hall, food to the hungry and a warm bed to the homeless. The new Church will be wherever and whenever we call each other to bond together, in the memorable mantra of my dear friend and guru, Davie Napier, "to work to bring an end to the terrible tears of the world."

With all this in mind, we can take a fresh look at what takes place when that community gathers for ritual and worship, to celebrate the Sacrament of the Eucharist, and how crucial that is to the whole Christian mission. On the night before he died, Jesus came to table with his beloved friends. As the meal was ending, he took bread, broke it, and said: "Take this bread and eat it. This is my body which shall be broken for you." Then the same with the cup of wine lifted up: "Take this cup of wine and drink it. This is my blood, which shall be poured out for you. As often as you do this, you will be remembering me." And note: It is not "as often as you believe this," but "as often as you DO this, you will be remembering me."

As often as we gather around the table in the Eucharistic community of believers, the risen Christ has promised that he will be present in this bread and this wine, really present, but in a very special way. Really present under the sacramental sign, to be encountered by us insofar as we can personally live into, and make our own, the sacramental words and symbols with which he gave us this gift. He guarantees that whenever I eat this bread in a "community which remembers," I am able to commune with him, become one with him, precisely in his body which is broken for me and for all sisters and brothers in faith. And when I drink of this cup, I can become one with him, in his blood which is poured out for me and for all sisters and brothers in faith, with the promise of life eternal.

SACRAMENTAL SIGNS EFFECT WHAT THEY SIGNIFY, no more, no less. There is no zap grace, no spiritual reality that objectively happens simply by spinning the prayer-wheel, by saying the words and making the gestures of eating and drinking. Our encounter with Christ is in mutual availability, and it is in community that it happens. It all depends on how available we as a community can make ourselves to the living Christ, who promised to be available to us under this specific sign: the sign of body-to-be-broken and of blood-to-be-poured-out.

How spiritually centered and aware can I be in that moment when I take the bread and drink the cup? Each time I commune I commit to break my own body and pour out my own blood in service toward the transformation of the world. Each time I commune I realize, just a bit more clearly, what it means to make my own the cycle of the paschal mystery of Christ: that whole Passover motion of becoming fully human, of dying to myself and breaking my body in service to the sisters and the brothers each day, and of living in the hope of rising again in the fullness of life that has been promised us all in the risen Christ.

The sacramental sign of the Eucharistic celebration is so rich that no one symbol can exhaust it. We talk about "serving Communion" or "taking Communion"— as if communion were a thing, rather than a personal encounter with the living Christ in mutual availability. All the words and gestures used in the rite are sacramental: they effect what they signify. For instance, as a Eucharistic minister places the consecrated bread in my hands, the words "Body of Christ, Bread for the Journey," or "Body of Christ, Bread for New Life," are no doubt true, but they don't help me fully realize the richness of the sacramental sign and what is happening here. This is not just cuddling up to my own little Jesus for my own little salvation.

EACH TIME I COME TO THE TABLE, I find myself having to add my own words, "This is the Body of Christ broken for me," and then "This is the blood of Christ poured out for me." I move on from there, not just fed by the nourishing food of Life, but also called to live into the meaning of that faith-filled affirmation in my own brokenness and in the broken world around me. This is a "missional faith community" that I am part of as I go forth from there along with all the sisters and the brothers who will join with me in working for the transformation of the world.

I am convinced that a new awareness of Incarnation and the World as Sacrament will lead us more fully into the mysterious adventures that lie ahead in whatever shall become the "emergent church." It is an exciting and reformative time, as we probe together with courage into the promise for the sake of all those who search together for hopeful light in the darkness of a faith that makes new sense.

ON MARRIAGE

| Ruth 3:1-5; 4:13-17, Hebrews 9:24-28, Mark 12:38-44 |

Robert Cummings Neville (2004)

BECAUSE OF THE CONTROVERSIES in Vermont and Massachusetts over the legality of gay and lesbian people to marry, or have civil or holy unions, it is imperative for responsible preaching to address the issues and not duck them to avoid controversy. I apologize to those who believe it to be unseemly to discuss topics like this from the pulpit, yet feel obliged to do so because of their deep religious significance and urgency:

The wonderful story of Ruth testifies to the profound loyalty that the Moabite woman Ruth had for her Israelite mother-in-law Naomi after the death of her husband, Naomi's son. In our texts from Ruth, Naomi tells her daughter in law to get into bed with Boaz so as to seduce him. Boaz, seduced, then acquires a field that belonged to Naomi, and with the purchase of the field he also acquires Ruth as a wife. The point of the story is that the child Ruth has by Boaz will support Naomi in her old age (and will be the ancestor of King David who is thus not a pure Israelite). Marriage is represented as the commercial transaction of buying a wife motivated by sexual attraction; the function of children is as much support of the elders as carrying on the lineage; and the only love in anything like the modern sense is that between the older and younger women who were in-laws through a previous marriage.

With regard to the legitimacy of contemporary gay and lesbian marriages, we need first to ask about that sense in which marriage is a civil union. The civil aspect of marriage does not require love but it does require a contractual agreement to function in society as a couple. In our society, the marriage contract does not treat women as commercial property. The marriage contract does define such things as tax status, rights to insurance, to health benefits, to disposing of estates at death, and to the care of and responsibility for children.

Like heterosexual married people, some gay and lesbian people, though by no means all, want to live together as couples, developing the domestic, economic, social, and legal roles of couples. Some political figures in Massachusetts who now oppose marriage in the full sense for same-sex couples have proposed to legalize civil unions that give such couples the legal benefits of marriage. This is the law now in Vermont. I see no reason whatsoever not to go along with civil unions in this sense. Viewed strictly as a civil contract, marriage makes a couple with roles of economic and domestic rights and responsibilities. If gay and lesbian people want to enter into such a contract there is no reason not to allow it. In fact, to disallow it deprives homosexual people of a legal right to enter into certain contracts solely on the basis of their sexual orientation, which is wholly irrelevant to their ability to observe the contracts, to benefit from them, and to contribute to society in the ways that justify civil marriages for heterosexual people.

For most people today, however, marriage means much more than a civil contract, and this colors how they think about the matter of civil unions. Let me attempt to describe this richer reality of marriage in neutral terms. Imagine society, if you will, as composed of a vast ritual dance of interconnecting social roles. I use the phrase "ritual role" in a Confucian sense to mean a general form for interacting with other people and social institutions, like learned stylized steps in a dance. A ritual is a coordination of many such roles in a complicated social dance. A society has rituals within rituals within rituals. Within a society's system of rituals lies a utilitarian core so that the economic, domestic, justice, military and other necessary functions are satisfied more or less. Yet the rituals are far richer than their utilitarian functions. They convey the emotional and value-oriented elements of civilized culture, providing both meaning for human life and ordered ways by which human aspirations can be cultivated and satisfied. A society's rituals are dysfunctional when they do not convey the intense satisfactions of civilization, including religious ones.

A ritual role by itself is a kind of abstract form, like the role of being a "student," which means fitting into general patterns of how to spend the day studying, having certain kinds of friends, dressing within the student dress fashions, living around libraries, dormitories, and the like. Each individual has to individuate the social roles in exactly his or her own way. No one is a student in general, only a student in particular, and many different ways exist for individuating student rituals. Personal identity cannot be defined fully in terms of the abstract ritual dances in which one engages, although that is the way we begin to get acquainted—"What do you do? Where do you live? Tell me about your family." Full personal identity is the individuation of those ritual roles with one's own impulses, chemistry, and inward life. In our individuation of social roles we play them more or less well, often very poorly, like D students.

Marriage in our Western society is a very complex ritual dance set among other social rituals. It has all the functional ritual roles outlined in the civil contract of marriage. In addition marriage has at least two more ritual elements. The first has to do with love, something more emphasized in the modern world than in the ancient Hellenistic world. Love begins as children feel themselves loved by parents. With the onset of adolescent hormones, love takes on an intense sexual dimension and marriage ritual includes being sexual partners as well as friends. Love also extends to the care of others the way the ritual says parents should care for children, with care directed in mutuality between the couple, and perhaps to their extended families, and also to the next generation. The next generation might be blood children or adopted ones, or surrogates in a host of other social rituals such as education by which older people care for dependent younger ones. The ritual roles of marriage are intrinsically involved in larger social rituals of care and dependency.

The second ritual element in marriage is that it is a fundamental defining element for personal identity: to be a person as one of a couple is different from being a single person, and this difference can be extremely important, perhaps the most important defining element of identity for many people. The religious importance of personal identity is that it is what we present to God. It is who we are in ultimate perspective.

Remember that I am speaking about the ritual roles, not about their actual individuated performance. In an actual family one or both of one's biological parents might be missing during the formative years, and whoever functions in the parental roles might be unloving. Love between the partners might be deficient in emotional quality or sexual fulfillment, and people's better friends might be outside the marriage; similarly a couple might be terrible actual parents for their children. One might individuate one's personal identity as a married person as a horrible marriage partner—abusive, codependent, emotionally absent, or adulterous. How people individuate the complex of roles defining the ritual character of marriage might be very different from what the rituals themselves call for in terms of ideal performance. Yet I believe that what I have described so briefly is in fact the cultural definition of marriage in contemporary Western society—a definition based on a ritual dance of roles for social functions, love, and personal identity but understood always to be actualized in ways that individuate the roles in better and worse ways. When people talk about the real meaning of marriage, they mean something like this.

The problem for our rancorous debate about homosexuality is that the way we commonly identify such ritual complexes as marriages is with quick images, paradigm cases or outstanding models. These images are nearly always too one-sided, too selective, to be faithful to the complex social reality. When we think of "captains of industry," the images that come to mind are usually of men, sexists as we are, not of women despite their prominence now in business. With regard to marriage the image, reinforced in literature, art, and tradition for centuries, is of a man and woman married lovingly to each other, each with parents, grandparents, and an extended family and together having children who in turn will mature and marry. This is the dominant image of marriage in our society. Even when we call to mind the vast complexity of marriage, and the distinction between its ritual roles to be performed and the actual performance of them, our thinking of marriage is focused and filtered through the dominant quick image.

Surely those people who claim to be social conservatives are right that few institutions in our society are as important as marriage, for purposes of domestic social function, the satisfactions of love, and ultimate personal identity. But social conservatives also claim that the heterosexual image of marriage is the only and definitive image of it. They believe that marriage itself, that wonderful ritual complex for human civilization and individual satisfaction, needs to conform to that image. In point of fact, however, same-sex couples can play all the roles that heterosexual people can in marriage. They can fulfill the contractual economic and domestic roles, the ritual connections to their own parents and extended family in learning love and care, the rituals of sexual love and fulfillment, the joining of careers and friendship, growing old together, and caring for the next generation, perhaps even in raising children of their own. No reason exists to believe that gay and lesbian people will individuate these roles more or less well than straight couples. There are winning and losing examples of both. I believe that anyone who can bracket out the short-cut images of marriage and think about its complex of ritual roles would agree that people of same-sex desire and commitment can enter faithfully into those ritual roles just the same as people with other-sex desire.

Of course most people are not going to think of marriage always with the analytical tools of sociology and ritual theory. We usually engage complex social realities by means of our images. Given the facts that about 95 percent of the population here and around the world is heterosexual, and that heterosexual marriage is far more efficient that homosexual marriage in matters of procreation, the dominance of heterosexual images of marriage is perfectly understandable. So is the passion with which those images are defended: what is under attack, as understood by people whose sole images of marriage are heterosexual, is not the mere image but the complex institution of marriage itself. Gay and lesbian people make up only about fivepercent of the population, and by no means all of those seek fulfillment in marriage. Very few models or images of same-sex marriages are well known beyond the gay and lesbian communities. The resistance to same-sex marriage, resistance fueled by very great passion, is a noble defense of the very important social institution of marriage.

But it is misguided, I believe, by its association of the ritual complex of marriage with exclusively heterosexual images. Homosexual images can also be faithful to the complex reality. In time, perhaps not too much time, gay and lesbian couples will be more conspicuous in the community and will be depicted in the media so as to take on iconic functions. For gay and lesbian people to be denied either the legal right to marriage or the social respect of being able to enter into real marriages in the richest sense is unjust. The injustice is based on a confusion of the heterosexual image of marriage with the actual ritual complex of marriage roles that can be played equally well by same-sex couples. Same-sex marriages do indeed threaten the exclusivity of the image of marriage as between a man and a woman. But they do not threaten the reality of heterosexual marriage: they only complement heterosexual ways of individuating marriage roles with alternative same-sex ways that are satisfying for people with same-sex desire.

A final point is in order to reflect on the Christian significance of marriage. The Christian gospel is that as God loves us as creatures in our own right, so we should love one another and love God. Jesus taught the ideal of friendship in loving communities as the best context for cultivating love of God and of the others in creation. No evidence exists that he thought of marriage as a particularly good form of loving community, and given the social patterns of dominance and the economic definition of women prevalent in his day, this is understandable. Our own society has developed to the point, however, where marriage, set in the ritual context of family, economy, and cultural life, is a highly prized form of loving community. To be sure it is not for everyone. But for those who seek to find their personal identity as married people it is perhaps the richest kind of community of love in our culture. Therefore, to deprive gay and lesbian people of the opportunity to enter into marriage and have that blessed by the Church arbitrarily betrays the Church's mission to foster communities of love.

Let us therefore bless those people who fight for the integrity of marriage in all its complexity, praising God for the passion required to sustain it in a consumer society that would sell it for a profitable mess of pottage. Let us bless those people who recognize that the image of heterosexual marriage depicts only one way of individuating the complex ritual character of marriage, a way fulfilling for those with other-sex desire but devastating for those of same-sex desire. Let us bless those people who provide images of marriage individuated in the multiple ways open to gay and lesbian people, and bless those who learn from these new images. Let us bless those who move our social consensus forward with patient but firm conviction to do justice to the gay and lesbian members of our community who are marginalized regarding marriage because our social images are too limited. Let us bless the God who forgives us our mistakes when we remain obdurate in the face of this injustice or when we push so fast as to threaten the social stability within which the precious institution of marriage is meaningful. Let us praise the God who creates from the depths of complexity in the institution of marriage, and yet who makes all things we revel in joy for life and love. Praise God! Amen.

THE REDISCOVERY OF VOCATION

| Playing drill sergeant on the road to a dubious Eden |

Jan Shoemaker (2007)

MY FRIEND, FREDERICK, WHO TEACHES LATIN at a local high school and who long ago studied at seminary in preparation for becoming a Roman Catholic priest himself, told me recently that there is a priest in Rome who has undertaken a job of a peculiar nature in the overlapping worlds of religion and art. It seems that some time ago—decades? centuries?—the penises were removed from quite a few Vatican statues, "if it offends cut it off" apparently being the mandate's guiding principle.

Today's more holistic administration, guided by their own lights, has good-naturedly decided to restore their manhood to these poor, cropped torsos, and it has become at least one priest's responsibility to identify matches made in heaven. Boxes and boxes of marble penises, corridors and corridors of emasculated, marble men. I imagine this lone priest moving in the shadows with his box of artifacts, holding penis to torso, turning away, moving on—God's own Cinderella Man. Good work if you can get it, I suppose—being indoors after all and including, as it would, room and board and the society of well-educated peers. Still, I have to wonder if this single priest, whose great contribution will likely go uncelebrated in Vatican history, ever questions his vocation at all.

I know that I question my own vocation from time to time—generally when the work piles up. As a literature teacher in America's public school system it is both my job and my privilege to direct what students I can toward the light—it has always felt like a vocation to me—great and honorable in its own right.

Nevertheless, when the stack of papers needing to be graded engulfs the banker's lamp I keep on my desk and laps up my evenings and weekends, I sometimes struggle to remember the purity of the call to teach. That's when I open the cupboard near the pencil sharpener in my classroom and study the two photographs snipped from old issues of National Geographic that I keep taped inside the door for just such emergencies.

One picture shows a squat, brown man clinging to the limb of a tree near a giant beehive as thousands of incensed bees swarm over him; it's called "The Honey Gatherer." Next to it a woman inhales deeply into the armpit of a middle-aged man in a sleeveless t-shirt. "Deodorant Tester, the caption reads. I study the pictures for a few minutes, consider the predicament of my fellow working class humans, and place hive and armpit next to my overloaded desk. To date I have been able, by this little exercise, to conclude that no, I do not have the most trying job in the world. A little perspective and I can meet the weekend pen in hand.

A little perspective is what I tried to give my sophomore American Literature students last spring when the National Honor Society came knocking at my door—those students who remained, that is, after a portion of the class had been raptured away to the exalted corridors of the NHS as its newest inductees. This is how it's done every April at my school: the club's advisors come right to my door and extend invitations to some of my students—one's who have a 3.5 GPA or better.

True to form, the Elect left my room the other day murmuring happily—it's so agreeable being chosen, after all. I saw them out then turned to the remainder, to those Left Behind, who to the last student wore the astonished look of the newly bitch-slapped. They seemed somehow naked and, in keeping with naked protocol, looked everywhere but at each other. It was heart breaking so I said the single, consoling thing that came into my head.

"Don't worry," I soothed. "The Army will be here for you tomorrow." Dead silence...then laughter, and relief. We finished off the hour by throwing around terms like "sycophants" and "anal retentives" and relaxed into the roomy remainder of the hour by putting our feet up on all of those empty chairs.

People will argue, of course, that these particular elect were not predestined to be inducted into the National Honor Society; in the course of exerting their God-given free will they worked their way there. That, of course, is correct—at least partially. And if you look at my little joke long enough it stops being a joke because what becomes clear is that, in lots of American schools—especially in city schools and in poor, rural schools—the Left Behind do, in fact, end up in the army. And that is no joke at all. Especially these days.

I have lost a lot of sleep over the war in Iraq. I was complaining about it to my friend and colleague, Stephanie, who teaches in the classroom next to mine, as we stood in the hall one day last spring while students surged past us toward their next class. We were both exhausted. Stephanie, who is one of those habitually competent people, explained that she'd been up late building a shed. "What kept you awake?" she asked.

"The government," I yawned. "I can't sleep anymore for hating the government." I know that makes me sound a tad obsessive—and not so much in a healthy marathon-running way as in a creepy shed-in-the-woods-survivalist sort of way, but it's true. I toss around in bed and watch the numbers flip over on the clock radio. At one-o-clock I close my eyes resolutely but there they are—right inside my own eyelids—George Bush and Dick Cheney, snug and safe at their opulent estates, with Fox News piped into their billiards rooms. As venture capitalists with the full apparatus of the American military at their disposal, they are probably a bit disappointed with the payoff on this little misadventure they've set us all on; who knew the Iraqis wouldn't play ball?

But then private enterprise is always a gamble and it will probably all come out in the wash—unless you're an Iraqi, of course. Or a member of the American lower-middle class who enlisted in the army. I recently read that one poll showed 40 percent of the American men and women fighting in Iraq believe that Iraq was involved in the attack on the World Trade Center in 2001. I know those soldiers; they sat in the back of my classroom and tried to get by without reading. They figured education had nothing much to do with real life—or with death. They were some of the nicest kids in school.

A few months ago I took a day off school to attend a writer's conference at a college in a nearby town. My daughter, Anna, who was a senior in high school, went with me. We arrived early at the auditorium where Thomas Lynch, one of our favorite poets and essayists, was scheduled to read and give a talk. Thomas Lynch is not only a brave and eloquent writer, a man of keen insights and fine, wry wit; he is also a funeral director in a small town outside of Detroit. He will tell you absolutely anything you want to know about poetry or embalming.

Anna and I, his self-proclaimed groupies—dead-heads in our own right, if you will—adore him for his gentle ironies, his tender love of his family and the hopeful and impatient way he looked forward to the death of his cat. We were seated in the front row when he stepped onto the dais and placed on the podium an essay he'd recently published in The New York Times, an essay that was pointedly critical of the president. The college is Christian; the crowd was conservative. I knew they'd all voted for George; I had their number.

I had been fantasizing, with all that time I had awake at night, about ways to bring the people in this room, and the 51 percent of Americans just like them, up short. I wanted to make them confront their readiness to be led by a simpleton with a simple message in a dangerous and complicated world. I had no clear end in sight; just a general longing for what seemed like an oxymoron: a humble republican or rather, a whole sea of them, shame-faced and sorry. I wanted to see billboards along the interstate that read: "Americans Dead in Iraq: 2,500 and counting. Halliburton War Profits: Up 284%. Congratulations GOP!" I wanted a bumper sticker that read, "You Don't Deserve To Vote Democratic!" Angry enough to scrap the greater good, I was a middle-aged poster-child for polarized Americans.

Thomas Lynch took a sip of water from a tumbler and began speaking about polarization, about the burden and consequences of our "fanatic" hearts driving us, as a species, into separate camps all over the world. He had me pegged; that much was clear. He went on to speak directly and softly and reasonably, in a way that could be heard, I began to realize, even by an audience who had not arrived ready to hear a word against the president.

What "I find most distancing about my president," he said "is not his fanatic heart...we all have that." I looked around the room; as far as I could tell people were engaged in a way they would not have been had I been delivering my internal invective from the podium. And then he went on wistfully to list the president's crimes against humanity: his lack of remorse for all the bravado and incendiary speech, for misleading us about the peril of weapons of mass destruction that did not exist, "for the funerals he will not attend, the mothers of the dead he will not speak to, the bodies of the dead we are not allowed to see and all of the soldiers and civilians whose lives have been irretrievably lost."

It was a frank and eloquent speech delivered to a quiet and, by the look of things, receptive room. What those people did with that message is anyone's guess, but to be sure, they received it. We were all subdued and thoughtful on the way out, and it occurred to me that, rather than denouncing the politics of the people assembled there that afternoon— as I would have done, Thomas Lynch had invited everyone there to see things in a slightly new way. With his gentle, sad soliloquy for the president's sins of impulse and omission he had made a little room in people's minds—enough space, maybe, for us all to sort things out and acquire some perspective. I felt my own fanatic heart soften, just a bit, and noticed that the people streaming down the stairs on both sides of me looked less brittle too—just a bit. I wondered for the first time how many of them had kids in the army.

Three months after that conference my husband and I drove Anna, who managed to elude both the National Honor Society and the U.S.

Army in high school, to her college in Chicago. She immediately began emailing us to complain that "readers," those people she would have something in common with, are hard to come by, even in the shadow of the Chicago Public Library—the largest municipal library in the United States, which looms directly across the street from her dorm. By readers she means, of course, those people who pick up a book like they take their next breath, as a matter of course, as a means of staying alive. It's always an education to find that the world does not mirror your own home. I see a darker outcome to what she simply sees as a troubling social dynamic, however. I see in it a pool of potential, unwitting soldiers and it frightens me.

In the over-lapping worlds of art, religion and politics, fanaticism of all persuasions often leapfrogs reason and analysis—I give you those poor de-sexed statues at the Vatican; I give you the Buddhas blasted away by Taliban soldiers in Afghanistan. What do those *madrassa* "educated" soldiers know about the world they live in, dependent as they are on the misinformation they are fed and the narrow perspective of the mullahs who "teach" them?

Even here—where real education is afforded virtually everyone—students too often choose if not illiteracy then aliteracy; they opt not to read, choose to let other people deliver their ideas to them, prepackaged like little TV dinners— Think Lite! "People who do not read have no advantage over people who cannot read," Mark Twain said—his words sprawl famously along the ceiling on the seventh of conservatives, a few weeks after we delivered Anna to her new college life in Chicago, I have been not so much restless and enraged at night as I've been deeply sad. The Bush wreckage seems too great a fiasco to fix. But here I am in the midst of another school year, and that doesn't leave a lot of room for despair. Yesterday when I looked out over my classroom there were thirty fresh, forward-looking faces each hour, full of hope—every one of them—for what their lives might yield.

Despite the weightiness I feel about the state of the world and the shame I feel over my own government's colossal, intrusive hand in it— putting on the squeeze, leveling other people's social structures and, for that matter, infrastructures, I feel something rising from the darkness inside, a shiny crescent—a slip of a moon. That's the real pay-off in teaching—the it's not too late glimmer that comes with almost every hour in school.

"How should I live the life that I am?" Mary Rose O'Reilley, echoing Rabbi Abraham Heschel, asks in her wise reflection, *The Love of Impermanent Things*. "Other lives interpenetrate mine," she sighs, "all of us struggling for enlightenment." A teacher too, she knows whereof she speaks. My business, as I see it, is to offer my students a thing I do not wholly possess—a room of their own, a spacious mind where they can turn a thing around and see it from all sides. Reading is required. Reading is patriotic. Reading is sexy, says the button I've pinned on the shabby old cardigan I wear in class. I'm a middle-aged English teacher with a formidable bun; what, I wonder, do they make of that?

Do I believe that I can solve the problems of Iraq, of Palestine, of Darfur in my sophomore American Literature class? Can I possibly counter the anti-intellectualism and complacency so rife in our culture, the "just tell me where to stand but make it simple" mentality that took us to war? I feel at once that there is nothing I can do and that there is everything I can do—that second voice is the teacher living inside my skin. We're just weeks into the school year, and I am astonished at the drill sergeant I seem to be channeling from my father's war. We're building readers here, soldier; drop and give me ten...of Thoreau's objections to his government. I'm becoming a bit of a badass.

All this attitude I'm putting out must be spreading around because reports are starting to come in. "You intimidate my daughter," an email I received yesterday read. Well, good then. And I'll not repent. Because it's holy ground we're standing on, boys and girls, the stairway to the heaven of the human mind. It's a dubious and obligatory Eden, at best, but where else would you want to live?

The old vocation seems to be kicking in right on time.

ON NOT SHARING OUR KEYS

| A lesson in humility |

Cynthia B. Astle (2005)

ONE OF MY PROFESSORS DEFINES "HUMILITY" as learning to see oneself from another's perspective. If that's so, then returning to college in midlife truly humbles me.

I suffered 30 years with a serious case of "education interruptus" because family needs, an 80-hour-a-week job and no money kept me from completing a bachelor's degree. In three decades as a journalist, I overcompensated for my lack by reading voraciously, amassing a trove of minutia that makes me a formidable foe in "Trivial Pursuit."

Thus I chose an interdisciplinary curriculum when I entered a state university a year ago as a "non-traditional student" (love that euphemism!). I also tried to curb my newsie's competitiveness in hopes of bridging inevitable generation gaps.

What I didn't expect was the animosity from fellow students over my Christian faith. The antipathy peaked this summer during a philosophy course on "Early Christian Thought," centering on historical-critical study of the New Testament. Two episodes illustrate my experience.

While we were reviewing differences between prophetic and apocalyptic literature, a classmate refused to accept the idea that "prophecy" or a "prophet" involved anything more than fortune-telling.

I tried to explain the Judeo-Christian understanding that a prophet is someone who calls people's actions to account according to God's notion of justice, i.e., that God sides with marginalized people. Referring to Nick Kotz's excellent new book, *Judgment Days*, I told how the civil rights movement was reinvigorated when Dr. Martin Luther King Jr. succeeded in convincing President John F. Kennedy to frame desegregation in moral, rather than political, terms—which Kennedy did in his June 1963 commencement address at Harvard University.

Even with a book reference, my answer elicited hostile resistance.

Two weeks later I tried to bring a believer's view to a similar question on the authenticity of New Testament stories. After I explained how constructing symbolic narrative helps humans find meaning, several classmates balked at the idea that Bible stories were anything other than fiction designed by religious powers to enslave the gullible.

The reactions to my Christian perspectives troubled me sufficiently that I went to my resident source of Millennial Generation wisdom, our 21-year-old son, Sean. We explored the issue while satisfying my curiosity about a new upscale, gated housing development under construction about three miles from our middle-class, ungated, racially mixed neighborhood.

Pondering the gentrification around us, I reported that a classmate had said she wouldn't accept Christianity because it "made my parents the way they are." Sean concurred: "Lots of my friends don't want to end up like their parents."

Nothing new there, I thought. I didn't want to end up like my parents, either.

Then my son pointed to one of the mini-mansions being built on quaintly named Coyote Trail. "If I had a house like that, I'd have lots of keys," Sean said. "My generation doesn't believe so much in 'me' and 'mine.' We think 'our.' "

Later I realized what a lightning bolt between the eyes his revelation was. The cultural mindset of my classmates, my son's generation, bespeaks a community in which authority comes from shared experience , not by credential or declaration.

Now consider two summertime events: a Virginia pastor's refusal to accept a membership, and conservatives' uproar over the Reconciling Ministries Network's "Hearts on Fire" convocation Sept. 2-5 at the United Methodist Center in Lake Junaluska, N.C.

In both cases, the rhetoric of those opposed to access smacks of "me" and "mine," as if the church of Jesus Christ belongs to us mortals instead of God. I feel sure that when such exclusions make headlines, especially online where many young people get their news today, a sharp cognitive dissonance results between New Testament instructions to "love your enemies" and contemporary Christians' documented behavior.

In other words, the shared experience of my son's generation says that Christians are selfish phonies who won't share our keys. No wonder my classmates scorn my responses!

My gloom lightened when I came across an online quote from an article written years ago by now-Bishop expressing frustration over resistance to change within his denomination (United Methodism):

"With Jesus risen from the dead, and the Holy Spirit loose, it is theologically impossible to deny the possibility of change. I realize, therefore, that my most trenchant criticisms of our current polity are deeply Wesleyan. I really believe in the possibility of new life, radical reorientation, detoxification and conversion. Don't tell me people can't be radically changed. I believe in mind- blowing, wild, born-again conversion because it happened to me."

If we truly believe that God's Holy Spirit enables radical change, maybe we ought to be asking more people outside the church how they see us. Perhaps then we'll detoxify our words and actions toward one another so that we behave like radical disciples of a Risen Christ, in hopes that others might see us and believe in Christianity's value.

Call it a lesson in humility.

REMEMBERING SCOTTY

| M. Scott Peck: May 22-1936-September 25, 2005 |

Lyman Randall (2005)

I FIRST MET SCOTTY IN 1989 through a mutual friend. At the friend's suggestion I attended the first of many community-building workshops sponsored by the Foundation for Community Encouragement [FCE]. Because of my involvement in a variety of FCE activities over the following year, I was invited to join their board. Most of my personal experience with Scotty came through this involvement, plus letter and phone exchanges after we both retired from FCE's board.

Throughout FCE's 18-year existence, Scotty often clarified inquiries about it by saying: It's *not* the Scott Peck Foundation! Nevertheless, FCE's life and trajectory paralleled his. After sales of his book, *The Road Less Traveled*, put it on the bestseller list, Scotty became a popular speaker; for several years he gave over 100 speeches/dialogues annually. This activity, combined with the several books he published during the 1980s, helped him rise to celebrity level, and he promoted

FCE in his appearances and books. In addition, Scotty and his wife, Lily, invested over a million dollars in FCE and its activities. As his energies and publications waned in the late 1980s and early '90s, so did FCE.

I once asked Scotty in a letter if he remembered inviting me ten years earlier "to join his church [meaning FCE]." He promptly replied that he would never say such a thing, that it must have been my imagination. It was as close to a scolding as I ever received from him. Scotty and FCE both became ambivalent toward organized religion. Although both got invited to work with many church groups during the 1980s, few if any of their efforts had long-term success. Scotty later observed that too few churches encourage personal truth- sharing essential for real community, the result being pseudo- community, not the experience of genuine community that most people hunger for.

Although he published over a dozen books, his most successful was his first, *The Road Less Traveled* [1978]. It sold millions, mainly through word-of-mouth. I would not be surprised if it is regarded 75 years from now as a classic similar to William James' *Varieties of Religious Experience*.

One of Scotty's least-known books, *What Return Can I Make?* [1985], was his own personal statement about his Christian experience and faith. Although now out of print, it's his one book that Zion's Herald readers might find most interesting. For reasons still unclear, however, it never developed the following that many of his other books did.

Scotty and I both dabbled in writing poetry and exchanged poems we had written. This led to my suggesting that we co-author a book of poetry, which I now confess was self-serving on my part. I assumed that his widely recognized name would guarantee publication of our work. Scotty warmed up to the idea but had two reservations. First, he wanted us to include a third author, someone who'd already had his poems published. Second, he wanted us to limit our search for a publisher to those he considered to be first-tier. We did find a published poet who was willing to join our project. We were surprised and disappointed, however, that no major publisher was willing to print our work. After our project was nearly three years old, Scotty suggested that it was time to "lay it to rest," which we did. The first poem in that unborn book was one of his:

Dancing
In the autumn of the year that I was three
My mother
Wakened me from dark sleep to see
The Northern Lights dancing in the cold.

In her warm night arms I danced to China
Before she carried me in.
I still dance, and I do not know
If I can ever forgive her
For such love.

At the final FCE meeting in July, 2002, Scotty addressed the gathering via a recording due to his deteriorating health. In it he acknowledged that, during the last 20 years, he had become something of a theologian. Although not a surprise, this admission reminded me of Scotty's religious roots at a Friends' school in Manhattan during his high school years. In FCE community-building workshops he often told this story: When attending Quaker School, I asked one of the elders what I should do during my first unprogrammed silent worship experience. The elder replied that only two mistakes were possible...to speak out of the silence when not moved to speak...and NOT to speak out of the silence when you ARE moved to speak.

Scotty was obviously moved to speak out of the silence of his professional psychotherapy work when he wrote *The Road Less Traveled*. Now that he has entered the forever-silence of death, he will continue to speak out, not only to me but also to thousands and thousands of others who are still learning from his considerable gifts.

COFFINISMS: A TRIBUTE

| Celebrating the wit and wisdom of a peerless prophet |

Stephen J. Sidorak, Jr. (2006)

A LONG TIME AGO NOW, at yet another stop along the national lecture circuit, a listener in the crowd to an address by William Sloane Coffin approached the speaker immediately after his presentation and pronounced the speaker the "perfect prophet"—because he got to "blow in, blow off, and blow out!"

I know Bill appreciated that response to his speech inasmuch as he repeated it often himself, self-deprecatingly, as he outlined his own sense of mission "on the road." For if the senior generation of Church leaders had to nominate for an Oscar one of their own for the starring role of best prophet, even an "imperfect" one, it would undoubtedly be William Sloane Coffin. Certainly a younger generation of Church leaders would also enthusiastically vote its approval. As a prophet to these generations, Bill has been without peer, both in terms of his capacity to "read the signs of the times" and his courage to "speak truth to power."

Now dead after 81 years, Bill described himself, right up to the day he died, as "an old man in a hurry." Despite declining health due to a stroke a few years ago and a long-standing heart condition, he still boasted of "flunking retirement." And while his heart finally failed him, his sharp mind did not. His penetrating wit and soaring spirit continued to inspire any in his company to the very end.

His mind? In his language incorporated into the 2002 Chautauqua Appeal calling for the abolition if nuclear weapons: "Indeed there is an "axis of evil." But it is hardly Iran, Iraq and North Korea. A more likely and far more dangerous trio would be environmental degradation, pandemic poverty, and a world awash with weapons."

His wit? In words uttered at Yale often: "The world is full of too many old Turks and young fogies."

His spirit? In words from a sermon he once delivered, "Musing on Mortality:" "Death is the great equalizer, not because it makes us equal, but because it mocks our pretensions at being anything else." Bill Coffin remained living proof of his fitting claim: "Being old is not necessarily the same thing as being stale."

Because of his sometimes halting, slurred speech in his latter days, he was wont to preface his remarks, at once a clever way of consoling himself and immediately winning over an audience, with the observation Mark Twain once made about Richard Wagner's music: "It's better than it sounds." After a visit to his cardiologist on March 25 of 2003, Bill reported the results, "about another year." Later, he added, "Doctors don't really know how long anyone has to live. Any doctor who tells you when you're going to die might be dead wrong." His response to his prognosis? "If I last another year and don't lose my marbles to another stroke, what can I be but infinitely grateful?"

His gratefulness to God for the gift of life immediately brought back to mind what Bill wrote about gratitude in his autobiography originally published in 1977, *Once to Every Man*, namely, that he always considered gratitude "the foremost of all religious emotions." I know Bill reassured himself with these words of assurance he offered others. "If we can't be cured, we can be healed. God is the only physician who never lost a patient." He was living testimony to his own intent. "Clearly the trick in life is to die young as late as possible."

Truly an amazing man, qualified to hold the title of personage, Bill possessed an irrepressible spirit that belied his "old age." Indeed, I surmise I was not the only one who idolized him.

Some of Bill's other publications beyond his aforementioned autobiography include two volumes of sermons, *The Courage to Love* (1982) and *Living the Truth in a World of Illusions* (1985), *A Passion for the Possible: A Message to U. S. Churches* (1993) and the aptly titled *The Heart Is a Little to the Left: Essays on Public Morality* (1999). His 2004 book called *Credo* should be considered required reading for anyone seriously concerned with public ministry, a volume that represents the vintage Coffin—the prophet Coffin.

His final book was published only last year entitled *Letters to a Young Doubter*, a veritable manual for the artful practice of pastoral care. *Holy Impatience: The Life of William Sloane Coffin*, written by Warren Goldstein and published by Yale University Press in 2004, is the definitive biography.

Probably the best introduction ever given William Sloane Coffin was that of his friend and colleague, Professor of Practical Theology at Yale Divinity School, Bill Muehl, at the third of his four Lyman Beecher Lectures on Preaching delivered at Yale Divinity School in 1980, which was entitled "The Arms Race and the Human Race," a theme Bill repeatedly addressed across the country and around the world.

Muehl began his introduction. "It seems as if at one point during their common lifetimes, Clarence Darrow and William Jennings Bryan found themselves on the same side of an issue of public moment. When Bryan was invited to Chicago to address the subject publicly, Clarence Darrow was invited by the sponsoring committee that had an eye to publicity, to introduce him, and he agreed. He went through the introduction with a perfectly straight face, listed all of Bryan's achievements, honors and distinctions. But just before mentioning his name, he put on an elaborate look of uncertainty, and turned toward Bryan and said: "Son— do you sing or dance?"

Muehl ended his introduction. "Well, I will spare you a reiteration of many of Bill's honors, achievements and distinctions, and spare myself the confusion, by saying with confidence: "Here he is, for his famous song and dance...." The congregation gathered together that day in Marquand Chapel erupted in uproarious laughter and sustained applause.

Coffin very much welcomed Muehl's introduction, in part because Bill had such a wonderful sense of humor, and was widely known for it. Let me illustrate.

Bill was an accomplished pianist who still gave recitals until recently. In 1956, he wed a woman by the name of Eva Rubenstein. Yes, her father was the great man himself, the concert pianist, Arthur Rubenstein. Now, the maestro was not exactly smitten in the same way his daughter was with William Sloane Coffin. After their first meeting, the virtuoso indicated to his daughter "he didn't want Billy Graham for a son-in-law." ""You can tell him," (Bill) answered (Eva), "that I don't want a Liberace as a father-in-law." (Fortunately she didn't tell him)," Bill reported.

When I had come to the end of a particularly difficult year, personally speaking, I called Bill on New Year's Eve to wish him a Happy New Year, hoping that 1985 would be a better year and expecting Bill to reassure me of as much. So, when I said to him, "You know, Bill, 1984 has been the worst year of my life," he didn't miss a beat with his reply. "How do you know, Steve?"

Announcing proudly that I had finally completed after twenty years of toil my D. Min. dissertation and would graduate at long last, Bill told me to remember "education kills by degrees." A man fluent in many languages, Bill was also the recipient of many honorary doctorates, including in 2002, the Doctor of Divinity from Yale. Thus, it is the Rev. Dr. William Sloane Coffin. So it warmed this strange United Methodist's heart when he left this voicemail message on my cell phone. "Dr. Sidorak, this is Dr. Coffin, but I'm a doctor only the way in which a gentleman in Kentucky is a colonel."

A year earlier, when word reached Bill at his home in rural Vermont via a phone call from a reporter with *The Hartford Courant* that George W. Bush was also to receive an honorary doctorate in May of 2001 from Yale and wondered what Bill thought about that, his reply, without a moment's hesitation, was succinct. "Oh, shit." And it appeared in print, spelled out just like that, in "America's Oldest Continuously Published Newspaper" no less! When I called Bill to relay this fact first thing in the morning, all I could hear on the other end of the line was a kind of vindicated chuckling. He would have the last laugh on "W."

When asked about forgiving our enemies as Jesus commanded, Bill answered: "Well, if you want to practice forgiveness, I wouldn't suggest starting with bin Laden." Bill's blessed sense of humor brightened anybody's day. He always seemed to have a smile on his face. And he knew the importance of a smile in the pulpit too. He admonished preachers, especially if they felt compelled to pronounce a word of harsh judgment on justice and peace issues, to do so with a smile on their faces. Aware that I intended to preach a rebuke from the pulpit of the National Cathedral to the Commander in Chief for his comments at the lectern there (a declaration of war, really) in the immediate aftermath of the 9-11 terrorist attacks, Bill's advice and counsel was sound and wise. "Give them—heaven, Steve."

Let me turn your attention now to the fact that no one could turn a phrase the way William Sloane Coffin could.

On the choice of presidential candidates offered the electorate from time to time, Bill was known to say that it is "not really a choice between the lesser of two evils, but the evil of two lessers."

On the "mediocre clergy," Bill is blunt, describing them as "the bland leading the bland."

On a more serious note concerning the nuclear crisis: "When we live at each other's mercy, we had better learn to be merciful. If we don't learn to be meek, who is going to inherit the earth?"

On Connecticut's junior senator, Joe Lieberman, who, since his Yale days, referred to Bill as his conscience every time he sees him or talks to him, Bill is unmerciful. When Lieberman learned Bill was not doing so well, he telephoned Bill to wish him well, adding once again that he continued to regard Bill as his conscience. Bill, exasperated and disappointed with Lieberman's positions on so many issues, particularly the Iraq War, boldly said to Joe: "Don't you think it's time you got one of your own." In a similar vein, Bill lamented Lieberman's overall political philosophy. "If only Joe was a Conservative Jew, and an orthodox Democrat." Talk about turning a phrase!

Another: "(A) prophetic ministry must always be ready to speak out clearly and pay up personally. At the same time, we must pray for grace to contend against wrong without becoming wrongly contentious, grace to fight pretensions of national righteousness without personal self-righteousness. If you love good you have to hate evil; otherwise you are sentimental. But if you hate evil more than you love good, you simply become a damn good hater, and of such people the world has enough."

And another: "(T)he best patriots are not uncritical lovers of their country, any more than they are loveless critics of it. True patriots carry on a lover's quarrel with their country, a reflection of God's eternal lover's quarrel with the entire world."

On Christian Faith: "Faith is trusting without reservation, not believing without proof." "Faith puts us on the road, hope keeps us there." "I've always been attracted to the recklessness of faith. First, you leap. And then you grow wings. And trust is a matter of flying a little bit blind sometimes because we trust that God is good and merciful."

On a characteristic he possessed, risk- taking: "Only those who attempt the absurd achieve the impossible."

And one more: "We are called to be tender-hearted, but also to be tough-minded."

reviews
rEviews
REVIEWS
sweiver
reviews
reviews
Reviews
REviews
reViews

YOU CAN'T PLAY THE BLUES
IF YOU AIN'T PAID YOUR DUES

| Review of *Song For My Fathers: A New Orleans Story in Black and White* by Tom Sancton. Other Press, LLC, 2006 |

John Winn (2007)

"I WAS STARTING TO THINK that there was nothing ordinary about these people. Whether rambunctious like Jim Robinson, or spooky like Sweet Emma, they radiated a kind of spirit that I never encountered before. There was a siren-song magic about their music that was luring me into uncharted territory. I hadn't a clue where it was taking me, but I knew I would not wind up exactly where I started from" (p. 53-54).

I remember some 50 years ago sitting in a hot little room listening to that kind of music, which still speaks to something deep inside me. It is "traditional jazz," the root-form, not what many people, mostly whites, call "Dixieland jazz." This had "soul," not just beat, and it emanated from somewhere deep inside, not at the lips or throat or hands or fingertips. Often the music itself took on a blues quality. Many of the pieces were hymns, with which the musicians, all of whom were black, were obviously well acquainted.

The place I was in is know n as Preservation Hall, a place on St. Peter Street in the New Orleans French Quarter, that celebrates and, indeed, preserves traditional jazz, the root form. I remember thinking then, "What a metaphor for the church: Preservation Hall." It was the title for my next Sunday's sermon. It was about the community that remembers.

In the midst of innumerable articles, photographic journals, compact discs, internet blogs, and books that have become a part of the wild wake in the aftermath of Hurricane Katrina, the one that stands out the most for me is not really about the storm itself. As a matter of fact, publication was held up due to The Storm so that the author, Tom Sancton, could add an introduction and epilogue as an artistic set of parentheses to the text that increases the universality of its appeal.

For many of us who lived inside The Storm, it has become a metaphor for all of our life experiences that deal with loss, separation, re-location, exile and longed- for resurrection. The invasiveness of it only cubes the effect.

Technically, *Song For My Fathers* is a coming-of-age memoir that becomes infinitely more when the unexpected tragedy invades its pages. The sub-title should not be lost on us: "A New Orleans Story in Black and White." Having grown-up in New Orleans and having experienced Katrina firsthand—and having had my ministry there largely defined during the black and white days of the civil rights movement—there are many touchstones in the book freighted with meaning for me.

What started out as a simple review has become a defining summary of my understanding of spiritual formation. Our own lives often come to life in another's memoirs, especially when stormy interludes of imbalance, crisis, and chaos occur that lead to self-definition and re-birth; especially when they tell of episodes which teach us how to regulate our reactivity to the unexpected, to what throws us off-balance; and especially when the life-experience itself enables us to have a vision of what might be that is better than the what is. Those are universals of every life story. They are what motivate us to dive deeper into our own selfhood. They are what drive spiritual formation.

Tom Sancton's father, Thomas Sancton, a sometimes antagonist to his son, was an alumnus and hero of the Tulane University School of Journalism when I was a student there in the late forties and early fifties. A star reporter with a local newspaper, he was often brought in to tell journalism students what it was like in the "real world." What we as students suspected and what his son, Tom, confirms is that his father spent less time in the "real world" than most journalists. His forte was fiction. He really longed to be a novelist. Nevertheless, at a time when there were few such white voices in the South, he was an outspoken critic of racial segregation.

Despite early, dazzling, success as winner of a Nieman Fellowship at Harvard, then managing editor of the New Republic at the precocious age of 28, and shortly thereafter recruited by Henry Luce to write for Life, the leading magazine of the day, Thomas Sancton by age 45, with two failed novels behind him and three kids to feed, was without a job. Worse, he had developed a reputation in journalism circles as brilliant but quirky, a talker, a prima donna.

At this low point in his life, he literally stumbled into Preservation Hall. The next night the whole family was there. It was strange place to be for the former Seta Alexander, Thomas' wife, Tom's mother, daughter of a Mississippi Supreme Court Justice, debutante, carnival queen in her native Jackson. But it was a welcome change to the long depression that had consumed her husband and her family. It was a turning point for Thomas. It was a defining moment for Tom. And it was "A- ha" for me.

Neither Tom nor his Dad could stay away from Preservation Hall. They wanted to be there with "the mens," as those old musicians called themselves. One of Tom's earliest childhood memories was being with his father as part of the "second line" at Papa Celestin' s Jazz Funeral on a raw December day in 1954. But it was those Preservation Hall nights that connected them to the roots of traditional jazz and to their own.

They had walked into what became a revival of the kind of music that is an American original. Until the 1950's most of "the mens" had taken on other jobs to simply get by. Many had laid their instruments aside, playing only occasionally. Most of them were living a hand-to-mouth existence. After all, they were only a few generations removed from slavery. Even the Creoles among them, and there were many, were seeing hard times. It is said that great art comes from great suffering: "You can't play the blues if you ain't paid your dues." They had surely paid their dues. But do you have a right to expect a re-birth in your sixties, seventies, even eighties?

PEOPLE LIKE LARRY BORENSTEIN, who owned the building that came to be known as Preservation Hall (originally an art gallery), and Allan and Sandra Jaffe, who later bought it from him and really put it on the map, began seeking out "the mens," luring them back to their musical roots. Without Bill Russell, a legendary figure in jazz history, there would have been no revival of traditional jazz. He was a conservatory-trained violinist from Missouri who later became the first curator of the Jazz Archives at Tulane University. He had much of the music recorded and preserved and was the lure that brought many of "the mens" out of "hiding." In the end though, it was the miraculous alchemy of Preservation Hall that brought it all together.

Fabled traditional jazz clarinetist, George Lewis, became young Tom's first teacher. He proved to be a fast learner. "Sweet Emma" Barrett, who played piano with Papa Celestin's Tuxedo Orchestra at age 12 and who proudly considered herself one of "the mens," said, "When you love something, you'll learn it. You've got to have the feeling for music and rhythm born in you. It is something you have to put your whole heart and soul in if you want to make a success. If you love music, you'll learn that horn." Tom did not just learn that horn, he learned them. As a teen he was invited to play with "the mens" at Preservation

Hall, the only white face in their midst and by far the youngest. Without diminishing the significance of his natural father, they also were becoming father to young Tom Sancton. He marched in Jazz Funerals with them and in the impromptu parades that are forever springing up in the streets of the Quarter. Back in the 1960's this could not happen in the Deep South without some ripple effect, but that did not matter. Something very deep was happening in Tom Sancton. His story was taking shape.

Spiritual formation or transformation, even, is not something we learn. It does not happen because we read the right devotional material or attend countless silent retreats. It happens in relationships. Relationships that are valued, with people whose well-being is as important to us as our own. It happens when we ratify their importance to us in some significant way. It happens when their voice speaks to something deep on the inside of us and we know that our voice does the same for them. All of that sets something in motion that cannot be unset, something begins to take shape on the inside of us that changes things outside of us. It is our story taking its own shape, not finished, but on course, not perfect, but honest, not slick, but faithful.

Tom Sancton is all grown-up now. A graduate of Harvard, he attended Oxford as a Rhodes Scholar. He has been the Paris bureau chief for Time magazine and lives there with his wife, Sylvaine. He would probably skip a beat if he found out somebody thought of his book in terms of spiritual formation. That does not matter. He got his horn out not long ago. Sounds great. It is his story.

One of the last of "the mens," Marvin Kimball, a wonderful left-handed traditional jazz banjoist and singer, at age 90, said to grown-up Tom, "I want you to do something for me, young man. I want you to tell the people that you played with me when I was 90-years-old, and I still have that beat. Tell them, please." He did. By doing so, he makes you want to tell your story, too.

THE NAZIFICATION OF ISLAM

| Propaganda film subverts rational discourse, feeds violence |

David Shasha (2009)

THE PROBLEM WITH PROPERLY ASSESSING propaganda and rhetorical excess is that often, in an attempt to beat back the dangers inherent in unthinking ideologies, the response to propaganda can itself paradoxically turn into propaganda.

So it is with *Obsession: Radical Islam's War Against the West*, a 2006 film by Wayne Kopping that was distributed last fall at the height of the U.S. presidential campaign and remains a shadow over U.S. perceptions of Middle East turmoil. Some 28 million copies of the film were distributed on DVD via local newspapers in selected markets by the Clarion Fund, which has links to ultra-right Jewish and Christian Zionist organizations.

Some of the basic facts behind the film *Obsession*:

- The contemporary Arab-Islamic world contains within it anachronistic and reactionary elements that proclaim violence

against the non-Muslim world and against even those Muslims who do not abide their literalist readings of Islamic traditions, both written (Qur'an) and oral (Hadith and Shari'a).
- In recent centuries Arab-Muslim civilization has had a prolonged and contentious battle between liberal modernists and atavistic traditionalists. The line between these groups has often been blurred with the institution of Western-approved dictatorships and/or kingdoms in Iran, Iraq, Egypt, Jordan and Saudi Arabia, which have formed a bulwark against both the modernists as well as the religious extremists.
- Iran broke this Western hegemony and marked the first time a Muslim theocracy established itself in the Middle East. With the fall of the Shah of Iran in 1979, a beachhead of Islamic fundamentalism was established, creating a new political template in the region.
- The greatest Arab power in the region in recent years has been Western-supported, autocratic Saudi Arabia, which has funded and provided a solid base of support for Muslim extremists.
- Underlying the new realities of the post-War Middle East was the role of oil and its place in the global economic system, which had been wrested by a new Western hegemony led by the United States.
- Unlike various reconstruction plans instituted in Europe and Asia, the Middle East was seen as significant only for its vital petroleum wealth. Regimes were judged not by good governance or for their democratic principles, but for their compliance with the new global Imperium.
- While Japan, Germany and Italy underwent an indispensable process of reconstruction after the traumas of a brutal war, the Arab world, which was just emerging from the foreign occupations of Britain, France and Italy, was thrown into a political maelstrom. That has now become a power vacuum filled with competing ideological movements, one of which is fundamentalist Islam.
- Lastly, the role of an emerging independent state of Israel in the

region has served not only to mark what many if not all Arabs see as a foreign accretion in the region, but as a symbol of Western hegemony which is thrown into the stew-pot of the political dysfunction that has characterized the region.

To the best of my knowledge, regardless of what one believes about who is right and who is wrong in the Middle East, these are facts that cannot be contested. The socio-political realities may be open to interpretation, but the facts themselves are not. Each of these facts is missing from the Jewish-produced documentary *Obsession*.

Using a canny mixture of incitement and factuality, the film's producers bookend their movie with the admission that the film is not an indictment of Islam itself, just a certain part of it. When I use the word "incitement" I mean to say that the film is completely disingenuous, as it offers a basic theme that it hammers over and over again: Islam is akin to Nazism, and the Arab world is in the grip of this Nazi-Islamic ideology.

Propaganda is a means to express an ideological viewpoint at the expense of a plurality of views within the parameters of open debate. According to this definition we can see a rationalizing process taking shape that stacks the deck of argument. To those living in the Jewish community, the primary mechanism for the distribution of *Obsession*, this "obsession" with Radical Islamic ideology is something with which we have become quite familiar.

Generally, the Jewish community has internalized its own expansive understanding of Zionism which is left unquestioned – often militantly so. Discussion is circumscribed and topics are delineated in very precise ways. Certain topics are deemed licit and others illicit. A deeply paranoid sense of the Jewish self is promoted; a sense of Judaism as eternally persecuted and powerless in the face of a litany of typologically-similar enemies who appear in a history that is marked by perpetual violence and persecution.

Exceptions to this rule or alternative histories are rejected with all due prejudice. The mechanisms of the discourse are controlled by social and economic means. Those who dissent from the accepted paradigms are locked out of the institutional network of Jewish organizational life; those – and this is not limited to Jews – who lock into the paradigms are lavished not only with praise and honors, but are provided the bounty and largesse of well-funded institutions which dole out funds liberally for those on board with the agenda.

The documentary *Obsession* is thus populated with people who are now sadly familiar as the "usual suspects:" Daniel Pipes, Steve Emerson, Alan Dershowitz, Itamar Marcus, Caroline Glick and Robert Wistrich. In addition to these speakers, there is also a cadre of Arab "witnesses" to the dysfunction of the Arab world. The Arab witnesses are thrown into the propaganda maelstrom. They have all passed through "conversion" experiences to the commonplace Jewish position after once being part of what they now consider the hatred of the Arab world.

This double rhetoric is an attempt to seal the deal. First, it is to be proven that the Arab world is Nazi-like in the sense that the nefarious Jihadist ideology has permeated all levels of the culture–a culture that we are explicitly told at the beginning and end of the documentary is not radical in itself. Second, this idea is reinforced by those who once served on the "front lines" of Jihad, people like Walid Shoebat, Brigitte Gabriel and Nonie Darwish, who as converts are best able to "prove" the "truths" the producers are establishing about the Muslim world.

Embedded within this discourse is a deadening and repetitive array of media clips of screaming, lunatic Jihadis and their minions. Image after image is laced with stirringly bombastic music that often resembles the propaganda that the film decries. The rhetoric of the principles being interviewed eschews subtlety and intellectual heft and hammers home in propagandistic fashion that Arabs are Nazis, and that's all there is to the matter.

Equating Arabs with Nazis, as the great Israeli scholar Idith Zertal has so brilliantly taught us, goes back into the history of Zionist propaganda–back to the Mufti Amin al-Husseini and to the Egyptian dictator Gamal Abdel Nasser, who predated Usama Bin Laden and Zaraqawi by decades. As she states in her book, *Israel's Holocaust and the Politics of Nationhood* (Cambridge University Press, 2005):

"The Nazification of the enemy, whoever that enemy may be, and the transformation of security threats into danger of total annihilation of the state, seem to have characterized the way of speech of Israel's political, social, and cultural elites, with very few exceptions" (p. 174).

It is not that Bin Laden and Zarqawi are not religious lunatics and dangerous fanatics who would kill anyone for any reason; it is that the rhetorical motif often does not distinguish between historical persons and their immediate contexts. The motif "Arab as Nazi" brings together Yassir Arafat and the Mullahs of Iran into one unholy cabal. As we now know, the deterioration of the Middle East has often come about because we are not able to see the differences among various Muslim groups and their ideologies.

The emergence of Wahhabi Sunni fanaticism in Saudi Arabia, the birthplace of Bin Laden, is never discussed by any of the participants in *Obsession* because it would serve to overcomplicate the ironclad principle that "Arabs are Nazis." The split between Iranian-led Shi'a Islamic fanaticism and that of the Al-Qa'ida-led Sunni insurgents in Iraq are very real things. They are not only ignored in this film, however, but are incredibly morphed into some monolithic version of Islam that is an *a priori* evil.

And we cannot forget while watching this execrable piece of propaganda, a work that is as unhelpful pedagogically as it is dangerous, that the dual logic of contradiction is continually at play: We are *told* that Islam is not like what is being shown on the screen and yet this is what is being *shown* to us with a relentlessness that puts the rhetoric of Islam as a peaceful religion to the lie. After a steady diet of one solid hour of seeing images of Muslims juxtaposed – *literally* – with those of Hitler and other Nazis, I am not sure if it takes a genius to figure out that we are being browbeaten into capitulation to hate all Muslims.

The "obsession" of this film is to turn the current situation, involving what are admittedly some very dangerous people, into a primordial battle being waged between absolute good and absolute evil.

In this sense, the rhetorical methods that *Obsession* utilizes to construct its arguments lead us nowhere. The viewer is taught nothing about the roots of this Islamic mentality or its historical connection to Western politics. The viewer is not told about Daniel Pipes' Zionist proclivities and the way in which he has reframed Middle Eastern history along the lines of those beliefs to disfigure and transform that history. We are not told of Caroline Glick's own sympathies for the messianic Settler movement and its belief in the sacred nature of the land of Israel.

Similar to the way in which Mel Gibson's hate-filled *Passion of the Christ* was screened in the fundamentalist Christian community, so too have the producers of *Obsession* marketed their film to the Jewish synagogues and Christian Zionists. The intent, apparently, is to create a grassroots movement of anti-Muslim hatred that dispenses with academic discourse and any hope that dialogue might present for a more peaceful future. As Itamar Marcus states explicitly in the film, there is no point in discussion, implying that all we have is violence.

The saddest part about all this is that the clash of discourses, the emergence of a moral Manicheanism that now controls most discussions of the matter, has led only to more violence and more dysfunction. I suggest that a return to historical and rational discourse about the Middle East might make us all safer and more stable as human beings living in a world that often seems to be flying off its rails.

DIGGING FOR ZION BENEATH THE SURFACE

| Review of *The Matrix Reloaded* |

Glen Slater (2003)

THE FIRST FILM OF THIS SERIES, *The Matrix*, gave rise to more philosophical discussion than any recent film. Several academic publications have been devoted to essays on its themes. *The Matrix: Reloaded* continues with this source of mind-altering experience and existential questioning. Looked at from the right angle, there's more here than one might expect from a typical summer movie sequel—worlds within worlds, religious allusions, and dark technological imaginings.

We follow the path of Neo (Keanu Reeves), who was "awakened" from "the matrix" in the first film. The matrix itself is a computer generated virtual world, so perfected that it is the world for millions of unconscious humans who are kept alive by an out of control technology. The trouble is that this technology controls all life—machines run everything. But Neo and his rebel friends, having discovered this actual state of existence beyond the matrix, are out to change this particular world.

Most humans are floating in vats of artificial amniotic fluid, attached to feeder tubes and electrodes. While their minds live in the virtual world of the matrix, they are really confined farm animals, kept alive by the computers. If you remember Hal in Kubrick's *2001: A Space Odyssey*, you might imagine what could happen if his psychopathic grandchild conquered the earth—it's a situation beyond the far reaches of Dante's *Inferno*. It's also the perfect set-up for the appearance of a savior figure, and Neo's mystical heroism easily takes us in this direction.

In the first film, this complex world was carefully revealed. In *The Matrix: Reloaded*, it is already established. So here the effect is not so much revelation, but deepening. We also literally plummet down. A colony of humans who have avoided the fate of the farmed masses exists far beneath the surface of the earth—"Zion." This is the home base for Neo and his rebels. The problem is that "the machines" are digging down to get them and something must happen—quickly. Neo must find his way to the heart of the matrix. The battle is on.

Subterranean Zion is a dank network of catacombs and underworld cathedrals—an engineered vision of necessity. Life is incessantly threatened, but there's community and hope. Most of all it is *human*, underscored by scenes of sensuous engagement and intimate relations. We get the feel of how humanity clings to itself when the chips are down. But it also serves as a stark point of contrast: Whereas those caught in the matrix are essentially detached bodies in suspended animation, in Zion bodies pulsate with longing, loving and life. The portrayal is one of great reverence for nature and instinct, which is obscured and distorted in any virtual existence. It all crescendos in a vivid collective dance sequence. The colony also harbors a groundswell of belief in prophesized liberation. It is the religious impulse surfacing at the limits of human endurance. As metaphor, the inversion of Mount Zion fits so well.

Zion's hopes are focused on Neo, whose powers transcend usual human confines, especially inside the matrix. Going on faith, trusting the unseen, and listening to prophets form the spiritual threads of the film. Neo and his companions share the capacity to function inside the matrix in a manner that is not so confined by its virtual "rules." But between this film and the last, Neo has learned to cut through almost every aspect, operating with "superman" capacities. Defiance of physical laws has become high art, not only slowing bullets to a crawl but also fighting off adversaries even when they come out of the walls en masse. In the world of the matrix, Neo is both human and beyond human, making him a fitting focus of the prophecy about "The One" (an anagram of "Neo"). The Buddhist notion of seeing through the world of desire (samsara) to the actuality of life—a kind of enlightenment—is well paralleled here, making Neo an "enlightened" one.

The now common sci-fi theme of a machine-dominated world represents the ultimate systematizing and dehumanizing of life, whether social, political or technological. Seen as such, futurist visions may be points of reflection on present-day trends: To what extent are we already slaves of the machines? How might the extreme imagination shake us from an unconscious assent to these trends? Beyond mere entertainment value, how might these stories awaken us?

To make but one point: Despite its benefits, the information superhighway, which increasingly structures our connection to the world, also presents the prospect of an increasing detachment from actual lived experience. Devices attached to eyeglasses that would keep us continually "plugged in" to "the net" are already in development. Chips implanted in our brains, connecting our neural system to the same, are on the horizon. To the extent that these advances remove us from our being-in-the-world, we likely will become removed from our deep natures. That is, we humans could disappear into a virtual world, and our souls may disappear in the process.

In Neo's attempt to undo the matrix he must see beyond the computer-generated reality and hold ordinary human emotion and sublime spiritual aspiration together. To the extent that he contains these experiences, using their combined power to beat the system, Neo's actions mimic a Christ-like task. That is, within the world of the matrix, Neo incarnates the presence of a redemptive power—"in the world but not of the world"—and moves to free the world from a dark oppression.

If these themes don't surface when you watch this film, it may be appreciated for its eye-popping special effects alone. The now famous slow-motion choreographed fight sequences are back in spades. Zion is itself a breath-taking scene, especially as its gates open to the inner-space ships returning from their ascents to the surface. Glimpses of the machines digging through the earth are chilling. A freeway chase sequence makes a startling 10 minutes of film. It is pure spectacle, if that is all you wish to see.

Scripted and directed by Larry and Andy Wachowski, *The Matrix: Reloaded* comes with large doses of science-fiction tension and drama. The cast is competent, but its members do not involve us in their characters beyond the mere lines of the plot. Laurence Fishburne's Morpheus provides the solemn, wise-man back-up to Neo, and the love-interest, Carrie-Ann Moss as Trinity, keeps our airborne hero grounded and vulnerable. Neo and Trinity's relationship, running throughout as a subplot, provides a heart-stopping (!), climatic ending as personal love is pitted against the larger situation. The story will continue later in the year when the third installment is released.

Spirituality in a big-budget Hollywood blockbuster may be cause for skepticism. But I'm a believer in the value of finding such currents in popular and unlikely offerings. Recognizing these themes wherever they might appear locates guideposts for an uncertain future. Seeing through the pitfalls of post-modernity to the more essential values of existence will preserve soul and spirit for the generations to come.

Let's not wait until the machines come after us.

WHY RELIGION MATTERS

| Review of *Why Religion Matters: The Fate of the Human Spirit in an Age of Disbelief* by Huston Smith |

Dennis Patrick Slattery (2001)

A WONDERFUL PUN ATTENDS WITH the title of this latest book by one of the preeminent writers on world religions., for what "matters" is the battle between scientism (or science) and religion, between the world in its material content and the "invisibles" that support and sustain it, according to Huston Smith.

His book is a reasoned, historical and passionate response to the legacy of scientism, which is essentially a materialistic attitude toward the physical universe that has most aggressively replaced metaphysics, (a much larger world view that takes in all those qualities and realities that science cannot measure or control). Smith believes we have been sold a bill of goods by accepting with little questioning the rise of a way of perceiving that ends with matter itself.

He treats this rise through a single image: a tunnel. Each part of the tunnel—its floor, its walls, its ceiling – is part of a grand historical design, which whether created consciously or evolved in succeeding stages, results in Westerners losing their orientation – the consequence of accepting objectivity as the only reality. Additionally, religion takes a big hit and centuries later, is trying to recover.

Consider Smith's chapter headings. Part One, "Modernity's Tunnel" begins with "Who's Right About Reality: Traditionalists, Modernists, or the Postmoderns?" then spends seven chapters constructing the parts of the cultural-historical tunnel that we find ourselves in. Part Two offers hope in "The Light at the End of the Tunnel," which carries the reader from chapters eight to 16, with titles ranging broadly from "Light," "Discerning the Signs of the Times," "This Ambiguous World," and "Spiritual Personality Types."

Smith concludes with an epilogue written in the second person challenging science to a conversation, for it is his conviction that how science and religion eventually "settle into one another" will determine the future course and condition of humanity.

Smith quotes the poet David Gascoyne to drive home this point: "The underlying theme that has remained constant in almost everything I have written is the intolerable nature of human reality when devoid of all spiritual, metaphysical dimensions."

Several forces have made this observation a reality in Smith's mind: Science's refusal to grant any secondary or tertiary qualities to the physical world since they can't be quantified; the rise of positivism in the European universities that we inherited whole cloth; the tyranny of the social sciences' heuristics, which includes positivism, reductionism, relativism and determinism; and the humanities programs in American higher education which have capitulated to skepticism wherein no truth claims are allowed. Instead, as Smith claims, a "hermeneutics of suspicion" is the guiding light in the dark tunnel, a light clearly inadequate to describe or explore all the dimensions of either the human being or the world's layered reality.

Theologians, on the other hand, have their own bat to swing; their claim is that there is not one but two kinds of truth: 1. Truths of knowledge derived from empirically-grounded reason; 2. Truths derived from faith, religious experience, morality, myth, literature and the arts.

On this penultimate point, Smith offers some incisive insights into the nature of myths, which he believes "impregnates cultures with meaning and motivation." He goes on to explore how: "If number is the language of science, myth is the language of religion." In this use, myth refers not to a lie, but to some revelation of a deeper truth that is not empirically-derived.

After a critique of the four founders of modernity's vision — Marx, Darwin, Nietzsche and Freud – Smith moves onto physics, and closes his argument by citing six things science cannot "get its hands on:"

1. Values in their final and proper sense;
2. Existential and global meanings;
3. Final causes;
4. Invisibles;
5. Quality; and,
6. Our superiors.

He states categorically that "the greatest problem the human spirit faces ... is having to live in the procrustean, scientistic worldview that dominates our culture."

His solution? Creating an EOCSR—the Equal Opportunity Center for Science and Religion—which would serve as a watchdog for the pronouncements of science and would create open spaces for authentic and candid discussion between science and religion. Science alone cannot accommodate the human spirit and religion cannot turn its back on science as irrelevant. Some détente is not only desirable but imperative.

Smith's urbane wit, his anecdotes, his humorous and often breezy style, are sometimes a bit cavalier, but never mind. He is generous, sharp as a thistle in his thinking and very accessible in his arguments. A "mystic" by his own admission, and an "open-minded absolutist" by his own category, his even-handed sortie into the genesis and rise of a mythology that is ubiquitous today, what could be called a "secular scienticism," is thorough and casual at the same time. His thought comprises a palatable, even entertaining journey through the forces that have benched religion as a poor player on the cultural field, in science's assumptions about the matters of importance and the absolute importance of matter, the material world.

Smith shows clearly how the great scientists of tradition were compatible with religion, and that the "religious sense" permeates the lives of every person. We should try to explore it as well, in a community with science.

WHEN LIFE CALLS OUT TO US

| Review of *When Life Calls Out to Us: The Love and Lifework of Viktor and Elly Frankl* by Haddon Klingberg, Jr. |

William B. Gould (2002)

DESPITE ITS SENTIMENTAL and lengthy title, Klingberg's biography of the noted psychiatrist Viktor E. Frankl and his wife, Elly, is an accurate, engaging, and well-told account of their personal lives that highlights their marriage that spanned more than half a century. The author, a former student of Dr. Frankl and trusted, long-time friend, is eminently qualified to write this biography with its many insights into what made them such a remarkable couple. Klingberg's conversational writing style, his affection for the Frankls, and his own experience in psychology and religion make this book a delight to read.

The first part of *When a Life Calls Out to Us* gives an overview of Viktor Frankl's life preceding his marriage to Elly Schwindt Frankl in July 1947. This opening section includes many vignettes from his early days in Vienna; a lucid explanation of Frankl's existential psychotherapeutic methods; an account of how the Frankl family faced the 1938 German *Anschluss* of Austria; his incarceration and near death in four Nazi concentration camps; and a description of how Frankl faced the future following his liberation from the camp at Türkheim, April 2, 1945, knowing that he had lost both his parents and his first wife, Tilly Grosser Frankl, in the Holocaust. The story of how and when he met Elly, their whirlwind courtship, and their marriage in July 1947, sets the stage for the narrative of their life together in the latter part of this book.

The second part of this biography, the life of Elly, from 1925 to 1947, shares material that has been little known to those outside of the Frankl family and their closest friends because of her desire not to take any attention away from her husband. As noted above, the last part of Klingberg's book discusses the events of the Frankls' life together, until his death, September 2, 1997 at the age of 92.

Klingberg is sensitive and skillful in interweaving the happenings and stories that Viktor and Elly shared with him. He also critiques what he learned about them from diverse sources, to include interviews and written material. His friendship with the Frankls has not kept him from presenting as complete a picture of them as possible. He discusses, in a balanced way, why Viktor Frankl was often opposed by others who included not only anti-Semites, but also Freudian psychologists, those in the psychiatric/academic establishment, and many who disagreed with what they called his "use" of the Holocaust in presenting arguments for his therapeutic approach to the self. While Frankl drew admiring audiences worldwide whenever he spoke, Klingberg notes, candidly, that there were others who disliked his personal style when he showed impatience, stubbornness and made demands that appeared authoritarian. Klingberg remarks,"Viktor could be variously, even simultaneously, strident and tolerant, self-promoting and self-effacing, harsh and humanely tender."

Despite the controversies about his life and work, Klingberg's biography shows Viktor Frankl to be an extremely brilliant man of great personal courage who, during his long life with his devoted wife, helped millions of every race and nation to find meaning. It has been said of the Frankls, "Viktor was the light while Elly was the warmth". Klingberg's story of their life together underscores this discerning observation. *When Life Calls Out to Us* deserves a wide reading audience.

short takes
Short takes
short shorT
Takes
takeS

RENAMING THE APOCALYPSE

| Preparing for that which can only happen once |

Joe Bageant (2008)

EXACTLY ONE MONTH PRIOR TO EARTH DAY 2007, I was standing in the coral sand of a tiny atoll in the middle of the Caribbean ocean at night amid several other vanishing species. Less than a hundred feet at its longest point, its sands were scattered here and there with the bleached skeletons of ancient lobster traps and sea turtle shells, and etched by the tracks and tailings of turtles, small birds, and all sorts of strange crawlies from the tide pool.

Swarms of translucent little crabs with huge black-and-white target-like eyes on stems coming out of their heads scurried furtively, avoiding the cormorants and other kinds of birds hugging the atoll against the same sturdy winds that once carried disease and guns into the new world and Spanish gold away from it. During the day the sun on that sand was blinding.

There was just that wind and absolute blackness with millions of stars and the cries of birds.

Never have I ever felt the presence of the earth's spirit and the terrible beauty of creation so strongly, where the world flourishes and struggles and dies right before your eyes. Thousands of colorful worms go by in the shallow water, winking on and off, and schools of tropical fish are plainly visible right at the water's edge, their fate hanging with the frigate birds suspended overhead.

And while standing there the wind rose and grew stronger. And as I closed my eyes against the billowing coral sand, that wind blew away all the flesh from my bones. Then it blew away the very bones themselves. And what I was left with was the core of selfness, just the awareness of awareness— the center of humanness that exists in pure duration before any thought or word is even formed, the unarticulated stuff that exists in the womb of woman, and in that great frothing amniotic soup of the mother of us all—the sea.

It was just me and the overarching black canopy of the world, as if god's own infinite bowl of stars itself had been overturned, dumping them upon my fallible and pitifully meaningless outer self—the one presently engaged in pompous scribbling about the liberation of man, yet unable to save a single one of those tiny crabs or glowing sea worms in the tide pools from their own destinies, from their return to the sea via the gullet of a vanishing petrel.

Western civilization began by smashing the faces of beasts with stones, determined to "conquer the wilderness," hammering at both matter and mind on the anvil of the millenniums until finally, we pulled down mountains and made atoms scream in tortured orbits.

Now the day of deliverance comes, casting our shadows in merciless hydrogen light, illuminating not only our latest war crimes, but also crimes of trade and finance and greed during what has come to pass for peace, when our darkest commercial cannibalism feasts upon the naked wondrous bodies of the innocents.

And now destruction dances in infinite rooms, singing in dark chords for the brute who smashed open the celestial clock, hungry to eat the ticking heart of god.

For all that the study of history could have taught an amnesiac

America about the fall of empires and civilizations, it is doubtful it can prepare anyone for what is fast coming upon us, because it has never happened before and by definition can only happen once.

Though the Wiccan priestess, the fundamentalist preacher, the rabbi, and environmental biologist call it by different names—as if renaming an apocalypse made much difference—we need a liberated theology, epistemology, or ontology (again, that obsession with naming rather things than doing things). Something to liberate "the within" of we who find ourselves traveling together amid gathering darkness toward the long promised kingdom of sanity and justice.

That's the kingdom which rests at the end of no mortal road, but was always within us—just like Jesus, Buddha and the Pentecostal preachers of my childhood said it was.

SURVIVAL OF THE FATTEST

| When in doubt about our future, try a little tenderness |

Charles Schuster (2009)

A CURRENT LINE OF THINKING these days seems to promote the idea that we are best when we are at our worst. It suggests that we are most apt to survive if we work it so others simply drift away while we save ourselves. People all over the country have decided it's time to pick up a gun, buy ammunition and prepare for the worst. The premise is that all systems will fail, and there is no systemic fix to what's wrong with us.

This mentality cuts across the grain. It exists on so many different levels that it is impossible to avoid it. Bankers are telling us to take our money out of the stock market and sink it into CDs – but we better be careful which ones. Others are harkening back to others times and places, advocating that we sell what we have, buy gold and bury it in the ground. You can order a package of seed that hasn't been radiated so that you can grow your own crops. Pandemic paranoids are looking for the outbreak of a killer virus.

Churches are being prepared to exercise restraint so that the best we can do is the least we can do as we make plans to don hospital masks, turn church parlors into hospital rooms, open our closets to store food, and plan *not* to hold large public meetings such as worship services. In addition, we continue to hear that the security alert is moving toward red, and only the strong will survive and only the fit will prevail. We are watching the sky for errant airplanes and scanning the ground for cylinders of anthrax. We don't know whether to look up or down, and we aren't sure whether we're coming or going.

If Secretary of State Hillary Clinton continues to believe "it takes a village to raise a child," and I hope she does, let me suggest the corollary: It takes a child to raise a village. It takes a child to bring a village to its senses. It takes a child to help us realize that the most important thing we can do for ourselves is what we do for each other and for our children, including those in our midst and those in our future. The measure of our health will continue to be what it's always been: how we care for children, the elderly, and those least able to care for themselves.

In an article titled, "An Evolutionist Looks at Modern Man" (from *Adventures of the Mind* edited by Richard Thruelsen, 1959), anthropologist Loren Eiseley objected to the evolutionist's proposition that we have survived as a race because we were strong. Eiseley suggests otherwise: "Humanity has not really survived by toughness in a major sense—even the great evolutionists Darwin and Wallace had had trouble with that aspect of humankind—instead, we have survived through tenderness."

On the 300th anniversary of the birth of Charles Darwin, and in the midst of a world economic crisis, it is important to revisit what has, truly, brought us through the fire, the flood, the terror, the famine, and the pestilence of the past. We have survived because we learned that we must care for each other rather than protect ourselves from each other. We have survived because we have learned to cooperate instead of compete. The human spirit has risen to its best when it has pondered the broad horizon and has been able to look past the tree that blocked us to see the forest that surrounded our pondering.

Eiseley adds great wisdom that speaks to our age when he writes, "Today we know a great deal about human evolution, but as scientists we have failed, I sometimes think, to convey successfully to the public the marvel of the human transformation."

For those who want to build barricades and hide from the masses, let us invite them out from the rock under which they are ensconced and join the populous to build our future, having learned what manner of greed got us into this mess in the first place.

For those who want to purchase weapons of miniscule destruction, let us invite them to empty the bullets from their guns and assemble to fight the real enemies of the state, which are found in the human heart, and to bear witness to the real cure for what ails us, which is also found in the human heart.

The time has come for religious people to be religious. The word religion is derived from a Latin word meaning "to bind together." This is a time to bind together even as segments of our population want to separate us from each other.

This is a time for the fittest to lead in our survival, but fitness is not defined by power and might. It is defined by tenderness and compassion.

That wise old fox William Sloane Coffin said it best:

"If we Americans aspire to become a more caring people, democracy and multiculturalism will more than survive; they will thrive. In this century we Americans have created a world for some of us; it's time, in the next century, to create one for all of us" (*The Heart Is a Little to the Left*. Dartmouth, 1999).

I miss him.

COLE PORTER AND THE MIDDLE EAST
| With thanks to Der Bingle|

John Lovelace (2002)

IN JULY 25, 1944, BING CROSBY stepped into a recording studio and, without having seen or heard the song, made one of his many successful platters with the Andrews Sisters.

Their bouncy little pseudo-western ditty, "Don't Fence Me In," came to mind recently when the Israeli government began constructing a 225-mile fence on the West Bank. The song title alone probably suggests the conflict between Cole Porter's lyrics and the Israelis' $60 million anti-terrorism barricade, but for those too young to have heard the song or for those old enough that the words may have slipped from memory, here's a sample:

Oh, give me land, lots of land under starry skies above,
Don't fence me in,
Let me ride through the wide-open country that I love,
Don't fence me in . . . .

Far from that wide open country, Jewish settlers and Palestinians both object to the plan to build the 225 miles of ditches, barricades, walls, sensors, patrol roads and other obstacles running roughly along the old Green Line marking Israel's pre-1967 border from the land it conquered from Jordan in 1967.

Settlers are opposed to the fence because they fear it could become a *de facto* border along the pre-1967 line in a settlement with the Palestinians, and they could be isolated or evacuated.

Palestinians object because the construction path veers in places east of the line in order to protect settlements or, because of geography, takes land they consider theirs. It would also block the estimated 25,000 Palestinians whom Israeli security officials say manage to sneak into Israel to find work each day, further crippling the Palestinian economy, already devastated by 21 months of conflict and internal road closures.

If Cole Porter's lyrics seem too lightweight for analogy and contrast, how about some plain talk from the poet Robert Frost? In his 1914 poem, "Mending Wall," Frost wrote:

Before I built a wall I'd ask to know
What I was walling in or walling out.

Fence or wall, the consequence is the same. Something (someone) is fenced/walled in; something (someone) else is fenced/walled out. Israelis have decades of experience trying to work it both ways: walls or fences to keep Palestinians in refugee camps like corralled animals versus gated communities, complete with walls or fences or both, to protect Jewish settlers.

In 1944, while Der Bingle, Patti, Maxine and Laverne were selling a million copies of a song about a fence, most of Europe's Jews lived behind fences or walls. Six million died there.

Can't today's Israelis understand from the Holocaust's barbarous enclosures that, ultimately, no people will submit to being fenced in? Some might even prefer the route implied by Cole Porter's lighthearted lines:

Send me off forever,
But I ask you please,
Don't fence me in.

faithWriter
FAITHWRITER
faithwriter
FaithWriter
Faithwriter

OF MOOSE AND MEN
(2002)

"The best laid schemes o' mice an' men/ Gang aft agley
An' lea'e us nought but grief an' pain/ For promis'd joy!"
– Robert Burns

To my knowledge, no moose has passed within a mile of any place I've ever lived. Perhaps that has something to do with the fact that, until a few years ago, I had never lived in Maine. However, now that I'm a Mainer, I should be ready for moose sightings.

When the day came, however, as it did a few weeks ago, I was unprepared. There, not 30 yards from me as I turned a bend in the little rural road where I was driving, was a moose. That's not what I initially saw, though. What I first saw–really–was a horse! Not until he (or she) made an abrupt left turn into the woods did I realize, almost too late, that I actually was seeing the profile of a moose (which, for the record, actually looked like two people stuffed inside an ill-fitting moose suit).

I thought of my horse/moose moment as I read about the failure of U.S. intelligence agencies to recognize an actionable pattern of events prior to 9/11. We could have hoped for better, of course. After all, these people are paid to detect unfamiliar phenomena. But I can attest that, even when the moose is right in front of you, so to speak, it can still look like a horse if a) you're unprepared to see a moose, and b) your angle of vision sees only, shall we say, the horse-like parts of the moose.

In the agencies' defense, it seems we moved sometime before 9/11 into a changed political and cultural world. Few of us in the West, however, had adjusted our vision to recognize life forms rarely if ever seen in our global neighborhood.

Who in Peoria, for example, before 9/11 had heard of Wahhabi Muslims? We're still trying to figure out if we know one when we see one (not everyone can be John Ashcroft, after all). But we have a general awareness now that there's a brand of Islam out there that is, in fact, hostile to Western values.

A growing body of evidence suggests that something similar to what happened before 9/11 to the body politic also happened to the human spiritual condition. That is, at some imprecise moment, we rounded a bend in the road and found ourselves staring at a set of circumstances we'd never seen before. And the effect of those circumstances is to challenge our spirit at least as deeply as 9/11 is challenging our politics and social structure.

These circumstances are well known and have many faces. They can be summarized, however, as two familiar crises. One is the environment, the other is the economy.

Regarding the first, ominous soundings regularly hit us like the slow drops of a water torture. From Rachel Carson's *Silent Spring* (1962) to the latest government report on global warming, we've heard it repeatedly: We're fouling our planet. Any single news byte about, say, industrial pollution may not mean much to us; even President Bush short-sightedly minimized his own administration's global warming report. But the cumulative impact feeds a growing awareness, based on facts, of our planet's increasingly fragile ecosystem and the future-threatening- damage we humans are doing to it.

Something similar applies to domestic and global economic conditions: The widening gap between rich and poor is attacking the human community like a moral cancer. On a day-to-day basis, many of us sense this condition without feeling moved by it emotionally or morally. The facts tell us, however, that an explosive tension stalks the world's societies and threatens to erupt, where it hasn't already, into life-and-death conflict between the haves and the have-nots. Witness the Israelis and Palestinians. For that matter, witness the ridiculous gap between rich and poor in America and the lack of tears for suddenly exposed CEOs.

Like 9/11, these two crises did not just spring upon us. The clues have been around for a long time. Only now, however, is a new spirituality or consciousness taking shape in response and challenging us to reconsider our tasks as spiritual beings.

The core of this new spirituality, regardless of the religious tradition, if any, from which it emerges, can be stated simply: "Grow up!" Grow up, and care for the Earth. Grow up, and heal divisive resentments. Grow up, and feed the poor. Grow up, and embrace diversity. Grow up, and share power.

At one time, we considered sub-titling the new *Zion's Herald* as "religion for grown ups." We hope that it might be so, but to claim such would be presumptuous. At our best, we remain a human enterprise with all the capacity for blind spots that accompany things human. With apologies to Robert Burns and John Steinbeck, the lot of both moose and men is sometimes to travel troubled roads, to fall short of where we want to go and to get a humbling surprise as we round the bend.

What we can claim, however, is a vision, a spirituality of growing up, that guides us in the work of dialogue and interaction with and among our readers; the hope is that we can learn better how to live in harmony with the earth, and not merely off the earth, and how we can live with each other, not merely alongside each other. Living a spirituality of growing up entails all the urgency of Jesus' call to drop everything and seek the realm of God – a call to maturity if ever there was one, and one as applicable to the body politic as it is to the human spirit.

As we should know by now, this is work that each of us accepts for ourselves. If we are waiting for others—politicians, preachers or stockbrokers—to show us how to grow up in the post-9/11 world, we're sure to see horses, undoubtedly some horse thievery, and even a few flailing guys in moose suits.

But one thing is certain: We won't see a real, grown-up moose until it's too late.

— **Stephen Swecker**

JESUS SAVES
(2005)

> "How many deaths will it take 'til they know
> that too many people have died?"
> – Bob Dylan/Peter, Paul & Mary

AMAZING, ISN'T IT, HOW LITTLE WE HEAR ABOUT mounting evidence that starting the war on Iraq was an atrocious idea? Somehow, the tidbits that do get reported on TV news or in national publications end up in the "Oh, by the way" category, rarely with the fanfare, say, of Martha Stewart leaving prison.

By any moral cost-benefit analysis, though, and no matter how the thinly "democratic" elections in Iraq turn out, we're in a sickening situation. It's one that should make every American citizen foot-stomping mad. A perfect example is the startling admission made to Congress on Feb. 17 by CIA Director Porter Goss.

According to the Washington Post, Mr. Goss reported to the Senate Select Committee on Intelligence:

"Islamic extremists are exploiting the Iraqi conflict to recruit new anti-U.S. jihadists. These jihadists who survive will leave Iraq experienced and focused on acts of urban terrorism. They represent a potential pool of contacts to build transnational terrorist cells, groups and networks in Saudi Arabia, Jordan and other countries."

In other words, attacking Iraq has not blunted terrorism, as we were told it would. Far from it. The war is creating even more agents of terror!

Plenty of us can claim to say about the war, "I told you so." But, what came to mind when I read Mr. Goss' statement was the final haunting scene of the prophetic anti-war film, Dr. Strangelove. It shows Slim Pickens sitting astride a nuclear bomb, waving his cowboy hat and riding hell-bent-for-leather into the sunset of a nuclear holocaust. Meanwhile, the music in the background is playing, "We'll meet again, don't know where, don't know when . . ."

If you don't get it (apparently many don't), the movie reminds us that the human propensity for war creates endless rounds of attack and counter-attack, with the stakes for civilization spiraling higher with each new round. Winning lasts for only a moment, but it also plants the seeds for the adversary's unending quest for revenge. And, so it goes. We'll meet again.

I've decided that we who regard ourselves as part of the peace crowd sometimes don't get our priorities quite right. Certainly our vision for humankind must be shalom, the welfare and healing of the world. But waving our "Peace" signs and marching for peace, by themselves, won't get us there. A prior and decisive step is the end of warfare. Peace- making, if it's to mean anything, works tirelessly to de-legitimize the culture of war.

As a species, we are beyond the time when a "just war" is feasible. St. Augustine, the father of just-war theory, could not have imagined a world with nuclear bombs, anthrax and Star Wars weaponry. If we as a species do not succeed in ending warfare, our penchant for winning means the human race ends up losing. War, to slightly modify Mr. Bush's rhetoric, must be taken "off the table."

Touching, but naïve, you say? After all, it was tried once. Remember the 1928 Kellogg-Briand Treaty abolishing war? Yes. I also recall that the next act of business by Congress after approving Kellogg-Briand was to approve funding for the newest generation of warships. The scoundrels were no more serious then than they appear to be today. Besides, busting our enemies' skulls is just human, a reflex. You can't change human nature. Look, if humans can make cannibalism, human sacrifice and ritual killing taboo, we can make war taboo. We already admit "war is hell." Who says we can't go all the way and condemn it to hell?

Against such protests, it's encouraging that growing numbers, even many who supported the war on Iraq, are horrified by news about America's use of torture. Now that we've learned about our government's practice of "extraordinary rendition"—sending prisoners to other countries to do our torturing for us—more people than ever may be ready to consider the moral and practical case against war.

And then there's the spiritual. Jesus on the cross inaugurated the end of war. In our time, that may be Easter's most profound and prophetic message. Accepting his cross, the New Adam, the "new human," chose to absorb death rather than impose death. By doing so, Jesus laid bare the truth of his teaching:

Whoever seeks to save his/her life by inflicting death in any form shall lose it lose, that is, life without war and violence which, unchecked, will end all life. But whoever loses his/her life "for my sake," i.e., for humanity, for the species, shall save it by ending the cycle of war and canceling the cancer of revenge.

The shorthand confession—"Jesus saves"—is literally true. The new humans, those who are "in Christ," accept their crosses and choose to absorb rather than impose death, all for the sake of saving not only souls but *civitas*, humanity in God's image.

The first post-nuclear generation of anti-war prophets— the William Sloane Coffins, the Dan Berrigans, the Martin Luther King, Jrs.—knew the path to peace required, as a first condition, the end of war. It's up to our generation—and the next and the next—to take up our cross and accept our calling. Ending war is the struggle of all struggles.

— **Stephen Swecker**

OYSTER ETHICS
(2007)

"God gave Noah the rainbow sign. No more water, fire next time."
— American spiritual

MY SECOND-MOST FAVORITE DAY OF THE YEAR is the day before the Pemaquid Oyster festival, an annual fall event in Damariscotta, Maine. I relish the delicious anticipation of what I'll be doing the next day, God willing: sitting dockside with my non-oyster-loving-but-loving-nevertheless-wife, gulping down the most luscious oysters in the universe.

The festival day, of course, is *numero uno*. I realize that, for the public record in a Christian magazine, it would be politically correct to claim it's Christmas or Easter. But, I can't think of a high holy day, or a low one for that matter, that has ever matched the oyster festival for the mystical union of the five senses that it evokes, and then some.

It's all there for one magical afternoon in Damariscotta: the clean, briney taste of Pemaquid oysters, naturally; the sight, smell and sounds of an idyllic New England waterfront. Sunshine, rain or the sting of a salty mist—it all feels right. This is fact: The Pearly Gates, themselves presumably born of the oyster, will be but a pale reminder of festival moments spent with my beloved—I holding a half-shell in one hand and a lemon wedge in the other, she holding her nose. Now that's communion.

Thoughts of such halcyon times have crossed my mind frequently in recent months. Summer visits to Maine by children and grandchildren from distant, oyster-challenged regions, though happy moments for my wife and me, triggered sad speculation for us about the world to come (and I don't mean the pearly-gated one).

If climatologists, oceanographers and Al Gore have it right about global warming's threat to Earth and its species, our eight-month-old Jacob, when he's Grampa's age, won't live on a planet that can sustain enough Pemaquid oysters for a decent lunch, let alone a half-day festival. And if glaciers melt and ocean levels rise at a worst-case rate, picture- perfect Damariscotta itself may not be recognizable.

Even the Bush administration, after years of denying its scientific basis, now concedes that global warming poses a real danger to the world, and urges that something be done about it while his tanking legacy can claim credit on its résumé. It's all talk and no checkbook, of course, but it does signal a welcome change in the public debate.

Sadly, even that smidge of rhetorical support might pass for moral leadership if not for the policy Mr. Bush actually signs checks for: war—at least $400 billion worth so far in Iraq, and counting. Furthermore, if he gets his way—and don't bet he won't—it appears that another war is in the cards, this time with Iran. The sorry fact is that presidents, as a rule, pretty much get the wars they want.

This state of affairs underscores two realities:

First, as long as we're susceptible to a war mentality and a president who wants war, we simply don't have the political and material muscle to fight global warming with appropriate vigor. Saving Earth, however, and not a phony "war on terrorism," is the battle of our time, maybe of all time. As secular prophets like Gore, Bill McKibben, Lester Brown and others are trying to drill into us, it's not just life in the suburbs that's at stake anymore. It's life on Earth. Forget the classic economic dilemma of guns versus butter. The truly meaningful choice we now face is between guns and, yes, oysters.

Second, Mr. Bush and other warriors of the nuclear age—the Bill Kristol neo-cons and their Institute on Religion and

Democracy/Good News chaplains—don't seem to grasp the internal contradiction of whispering about the environment while blowing bugles for wars of aggression and "keeping all options on the table," including the use of nuclear weapons. They don't dare tell the dirty truth: War and the war industry are the ultimate polluters.

It has come to this: War as an option for settling conflict has but one evolutionary trajectory, i.e., destruction of the environment and the human habitat. The military- industrial complex is not merely a socio-political apparatus to be feared for democracy's sake, as President Eisenhower warned. It's also the consummate threat to the global environment. We're just one devastating nuclear bomb away from "the fire next time" through which, our ancestors predict, the divine judgment will make its final appearance.

It would be tragic irony if the Culture Wars of the last 50 years were to morph into a totalitarian Culture of War during the next 50 years. Based on historical trends, though, it could happen to America just as it did to Rome. But, is anyone asking the current crop of political candidates whether they intend to oppose that culture? Or asking them what wars they want to start? If not, by what measure can we know where we may be headed, the consequences we face and what can be done to change course before it's too late?

As anticipated, the recent oyster festival was stupendous. The combination of superb bivalve mollusks, an indulgent spouse and an amazing Johnny Cash sound-alike exuded soul. For the moment, at least, it renewed my hope in a God that surely loves oysters (in a Creator sort of way, of course) as much as I do.

— **Stephen Swecker**

GIMME COD
(2009)

"A thousand ages, in thy sight, are like an evening gone ..."
– Isaac Watts, based on Psalm 90 (1719)

As DAVID BODANIS SHOWS in his sparkling book on the history of electricity (*Electric Universe*, Three Rivers Press, 2005), the speed with which information moved prior to the early 19th century had not changed for thousands of years. In essence, it was limited by how fast your horse could run, the prevailing weather conditions and the endurance of the rider carrying the message. Suddenly, with the invention of the telegraph, all that changed. With the click of a key, an operator in Boston could transmit the price of fish to a buyer in Philadelphia faster than the buyer could say "gimme some cod."

Think of it: That was less than a mere 200 years ago. Some of us reading this magazine have grandparents who were born before the telegraph's invention – who were alive, that is, in the era when a fast horse was the iPhone of its day. And a long era it was. It comprised all of human history up until that decisive moment in 1844 when Samuel Morse first demonstrated the telegraph's commercial value as a means of communication.

I can't think of more powerful imagery for capturing how different our world is from the world of our relatively recent ancestors, that is, prior to 1800. What we have in common with them is considerable, of course, and of abiding worth to our understanding of human life. But, in 200 years, a historical blink, the speed and the ways by which we communicate with each other have altered nearly every aspect of our life – from how we travel, to how we eat, to how we entertain ourselves, to how we talk (Google, anyone?).

Until 1844, the way forward was reasonably assured. After all, the world had been virtually the same year after year – a gradual, incrementally-changing flow, moving at a familiar and constant speed – for as long as anyone could remember. But, when the velocity with which information could move from place to place approached the speed of light, the world itself went into turbo drive.

To switch metaphors, until 1800 or so, the human race was on a slow, steady uphill climb of a rollercoaster that hadn't yet started downhill. Since then, we've been in a dizzying plunge of constant, mind-boggling change. The ride has been exhilarating. The problem is that no one looked ahead and warned us about the sudden stop at the end. Whoops.

Okay, I don't know if we're at that precise point. Apocalyptic isn't my game. As far as we know, the sun will come up tomorrow and the stock market will open on time. But, when we learn as we did one day last month that two satellites – one Russian, the other American – crashed in orbit, spraying hi-tech debris into the paths of other satellites, we sense that the roller coaster we're riding may itself be entering a fateful collision zone.

As a classic George Carlin comedy routine illustrated a few decades ago, maybe we've crossed a threshold in our fanatic, speed-driven need to produce and acquire "stuff." If space itself is now so crowded that our stuff "up there" is bumping into itself, how precariously overstuffed have we become "down here" on Earth? Nobody knows. Really, it all happened so fast. Ol' Sam Morse started clicking away one day, and we've been on a hair-raising ride ever since.

Who knows if it's too late to slow things down? Even our new president, who seems like a refreshingly mature fellow, has been flooring the throttle on matters of state. He seems to think time is running out for meaningful legislative action. He may be right, but how would we know? We're all high on speed and, one fears, severely impaired in our judgments about what is best for ourselves, let alone the country and world.

What we need here is some perspective, the kind religion at its best once supplied. Perspective is hard to come by, however, when anxiety about the economy – particularly our personal economy – is running high. One even wonders how religion itself has been affected by the breakneck pace of modern life. Might it, too, be on a collision course – the so-called "clash of civilizations" –and destined, like satellites in space, to throw off hazardous bits of spiritual shrapnel into the path of a whirring humanity?

Perhaps it is time to pull back from the wreckage and assess what we have come to as the species in charge of Earth (or are we)? Passover and Easter, seasons of deep reflection for Jews and Christians, loom. Together they provide an opening for pondering what has happened to us during the past 200 years and what to do to re-gain our moral, spiritual and existential bearings before the whole shebang spins out of control.

It's time, in other words, to send ourselves a SOS – but not by telegraph. Too slow.

— **Stephen Swecker**

Special Report

FOLLOW THE MONEY
| The Right's well-heeled assault on the UMC |

Andrew J. Weaver and Nicole Seibert (2006)

SIX MONTHS AGO, WE REVIEWED in these pages an unsettling book titled *United Methodism@Risk: A Wake Up Call* by Leon Howell (see *Zion's Herald*, July/August 2003). The book exposes an orchestrated attack by the American political and religious right on The United Methodist Church (UMC) and other mainline Protestant denominations that have been sufficiently vigorous, socially involved and politically effective to garner its wrath (Howell, 2003).

In response to the ensuing criticism of the book and our review, we organized a group of researchers to check the facts and found the volume to be well documented and reliable. In the process, we also reviewed hundreds of documents published by the key organization involved in the assault on the church, namely, the Institute on Religion and Democracy (IRD). Our findings outlined below are very disturbing.

The IRD is affiliated with no denomination and is only accountable to its own self-appointed, self-perpetuating board of directors. According to public sources, the IRD focuses its principal expenditures and most of its efforts on The United Methodist Church. In 2001, it spent $358,667 (46 percent of its total program expenditures) on "monitoring" the UMC's activities, leadership and public policy statements. In 1999, it spent $337,636 for the same purpose – more than six times what it spent on its "religious liberty" program that it declares in IRS documents to be its primary purpose (Taylor, 2003).

From its inception in 1982, IRD has been generously funded primarily by ultra-conservative organizations (Media Transparency, 2003). Records show that since it was founded, the IRD has received more than $1.9 million from the Scaife foundations, including an initial start-up grant of $200,000 (The Public Eye, 1989). The Scaife Family Foundations, managed by Richard Mellon Scaife, gave $225,000 to the IRD in 2002 for its "Reforming America's Churches Project" – among whose stated goals is the elimination of the UMC's General Board of Church and Society, the church's voice for justice and peace, as well as discrediting UMC pastors and bishops with whom they disagree by instigating church trials (Information Project for United Methodists, 2003). With respect to church trials, the IRD states the following in a fund-raising document to donors: "Over the next three years, we expect involvement in at least a dozen different cases around the country" (Institute on Religion and Democracy, 2001a).

The significance of the Scaife family's support of the IRD is best understood in the context of their foundations' overall pattern of funding. Richard Mellon Scaife, who controls the foundations' funds, is a billionaire who has subsidized many of the political right's formative institutions and organizations during the past 30 years (Rothmyer, 2000). His wealth was inherited from the Mellon banking and oil fortune.

In 1999 equivalent dollars, the *Washington Post* calculated that Mr. Scaife gave to conservative causes and institutions some $620 million during that 30-year period (Kaiser & Chinoy, 1999). In the 1990s, Mr. Scaife supported groups with millions of dollars to fund lawsuits against the Clinton administration on a multitude of issues. In a revealing interview in 1999 with John F. Kennedy, Jr., in *George Magazine*, Mr. Scaife claimed that the Clintons were involved in the deaths of 60 friends and employees – bizarre accusations that have never been taken seriously in a court of law nor been shown to have a basis in fact (Kennedy, 1999).

THE SCAIFE FAMILY, HOWEVER, IS NOT ALONE in funding the IRD. California-based Fieldstead and Company is the conduit for the interests of Howard Fieldstead Ahmanson, whose father amassed a fortune in the savings-and-loan industry. Howard Ahmanson and his wife, Roberta, who serves on the IRD board of directors, have been key supporters of Chalcedon Inc., the Christian Reconstructionist think tank where Howard Ahmanson served on the board of directors for 23 years (Olsen, 1998). Christian Reconstructionism is a hard-line Calvinist movement that advocates replacing American democracy with a fundamentalist theocracy under strict biblical codes. For example, they would impose the death penalty "by stoning" on everyone from adulterers and homosexuals to incorrigible children and those who spread "false" religions (Robinson, 2002). Ahmanson gave IRD $58,960 in 1991 and $234,135 in 1992 (Howell, 1995) and according to an IRD disclosure recently made to the *Washington Post*, Ahmanson continues to give on average $75,000 a year (Cooperman, 2003).

Other IRD funding sources include the John M. Olin Foundation, whose namesake manufactured Winchester rifles; Olin has backed the IRD in the amount of $489,000 "to counter the political influence of the Religious Left." The Castle Rock Foundation, created by the Adolph Coors family in 1993, gave $90,000 to IRD to "challenge the orthodoxy promoted by liberal religious leaders in the U.S." The Lynde and Harry Bradley Foundation, funded by a family with ties to the ultra-conservative John Birch Society, gave $1.5 million between 1985 and 2001 to IRD efforts (Media Transparency, 2003). The Bradley Foundation's stated objective is to return the U.S. to the days before government regulated business and corporations were required to negotiate with labor unions (Media Transparency, 2003).

How significant is the relationship between the IRD and this secular-funding base? Between 1985-2002, the IRD ranked 81st in money received on a list of 2609 recipients of funding from right-wing organizations (Media Transparency, 2003). The National Committee for Responsive Philanthropy published a report in 1997 showing how a dozen foundations have prevailed in shaping public policy. It found that the organizations that fund the IRD (and a few others) diverge in their practices from the generally accepted social and ethical norms of the philanthropic sector (National Committee for Responsive Philanthropy, 1997). According to this report, the IRD-supporting foundations' agendas include the aggressive furthering of public policy that favors the wealthy and the use of government power to support corporate interests and *laissez-faire* capitalism (Media Transparency, 2003).

What does this all mean? At the very least, we can say that the IRD, by uncritically accepting funds from such organizations, tacitly approves of their agendas. Conversely, it would appear obvious that the IRD would not receive funding from such groups were it opposed to their objectives.

The IRD's stated goals, which consistently are at odds with the historic social witness of the mainline churches, include increasing military spending, opposing environmental protection efforts and eliminating social welfare programs (Institute on Religion and Democracy, 2001a). In this respect, it can be said that the IRD and its wealthy patrons are intent on derailing if not outright controlling the UMC's social witness. If that sounds implausible, one need only consider how right-wing groups during the last decade have done that and more in their take-over of the Southern Baptist Convention.

HOW DO THEY OPERATE in pursuit of their goals? The IRD's *modus operandi* is to vilify and ridicule UMC officials, organizations and programs that do not reflect its views. For example, in March of 2001, the IRD demonstrated utter contempt for United Methodist bishops in an assault on their collective judgment and integrity; this was published on the *Good News* Web site under the title, "The Methodist President and His Bishops" (Tooley, 2001a). Mark Tooley, executive director of IRD's United Methodist monitoring program, a former CIA analyst and a board member of Good News, called the bishops *en masse* "fatuous" and "pompous." According to Mr. Tooley, "statements from United

Methodist bishops are often inarticulate and sometimes downright nonsensical." He was particularly agitated by their unanimous vote questioning the proposed expenditure of tens of billions of dollars by the Bush Administration on a "Star Wars" missile defense system that is without proven scientific merit (PBS, 2003). He also was scornful of the bishops when they expressed concern for "children and the poor," who, according to the bishops, are being impoverished as a result of excessive military expenditures (Tooley, 2001a).

The IRD hardly has a good word to say about any United Methodist leaders. For example, when Duke University adopted a policy (supported by both North Carolina bishops) that students and their families could use the university chapel for same-sex blessings by churches that permit them, Mr. Tooley and the IRD unleashed an attack on the Rev. Dr. William Willimon (Willimon, 2001). Dr. Willimon is the Dean of the Chapel at Duke and a widely respected leader within the UMC community and beyond. When he contacted the IRD to report that he and his secretary were receiving hate mail and pornographic materials in the name of the IRD's protest, Mr. Tooley wrote back saying, "If you can't take the heat, get out of the kitchen." Mr. Tooley stated that he had no interest in talking further with Dr. Willimon until he resigned from Duke (Willimon, 2003).

Dr. Willimon is in good company. IRD has attacked, among others, Archbishop Desmond Tutu, Rev. Jim Wallis of Sojourners, the evangelical leader Dr. Tony Campolo, the National Council of Catholic Bishops, the UMC's Igniting Ministry public relations campaign (Bowdon, 2001), the UMC's newest hymnal (McIntyre, 2001) and numerous other distinguished Protestant, Catholic, and Jewish leaders and programs ("United Methodists Affirming Christ's Teachings in our Nation, 2003;" UM Action, 2000).

There's more. For example, when the Interfaith Alliance was formed during the 1990s as a progressive multi-faith group to counter the bullying of the Christian Coalition and others on the religious right, Mr. Tooley took exception. He was upset that prominent and respected Americans like Walter Cronkite were trying to help the multi-faith group (Neuhaus, 1997). Perhaps harking back to his cold-warrior days in the

CIA, Mr. Tooley likened several Christian and Jewish leaders to communist stooges: "The Interfaith Alliance's board is about as diverse as a Soviet politburo during the empire's final, geriatric years. Yes, some were bald, others had bushy eyebrows. Some came from Leningrad, others from Minsk. Some were septuagenarians, others were octogenarians ... There are two Catholic bishops from the church's left-fringe. Three liberal rabbis. And several Black denominational leaders who shun the social conservatism typical of most black churches" (Neuhaus, 1997).

Of course, he is belittling some of the most eminent religious leaders in America who serve on the Interfaith Alliance Board, including Rabbi David Gelfand, Senior Rabbi at The Jewish Center of the Hamptons in East Hampton, New York; Rev. Gardner C. Taylor, Pastor Emeritus of the Concord Baptist Church of Christ in Brooklyn, and past president of the Progressive National Baptist Convention; and Dr. J. Philip Wogaman, former Dean of Wesley Seminary in Washington, D.C. and retired Senior Minister of Foundry UMC in the nation's capitol (The Interfaith Alliance, 2003).

MR. TOOLEY IS NOT ALONE, HOWEVER. Diane Knippers, formerly a United Methodist, is now a member of the Truro Episcopal Church in Fairfax, Virginia (along with Colonel Oliver North) and heads up the IRD. Ms. Knippers recently made the claim in The United Methodist Reporter that "The fact is that the IRD rarely takes any kind of political position" (Smith, 2002). Nothing could be further from the truth. It would be difficult to find a right-wing Republican position that IRD has not rallied behind with gusto. We documented several dozen examples. Following are only a few.

The IRD has pressed the Bush administration to take a harder line on North Korea (Goodenough, 2003) and vigorously supported Republican tax cuts for the rich (Tooley, 2001b, c). Mr. Tooley's direct board of directors supervisor, David Stanley, is the chairman of a radical anti-tax group (Clark, 1999) that advocates the slashing of government services for the poor and disabled and huge tax cuts for the wealthy (Neas, 2003). The IRD opposes even limited environmental protection efforts and has collaborated with other like-minded folks to try to roll back protections now in place (Interfaith Coalition for Environmental Stewardship, 2003; Public Eye, 2003; Sider & Ball, 2002; Tooley, 2002). The IRD, particularly Ms. Knippers, has been vocal in opposition to any form of hate crime legislation (Jones, 2000). It has expressed opposition to a land mines treaty (Institute on Religion and Democracy, 2001b) and to women even having knowledge about reproductive choices (Institute on Religion and Democracy, 2001c).

Further illustrating its political stands, when Dr. Richard Land, former teacher at Criswell College in Dallas and now president of the Southern Baptist Convention's Ethics and Religious Liberty Commission, spoke out in September 2002 for a preemptive war on Iraq, IRD was virtually the only other "religious" group in America that backed the idea (McMullen, 2002). Even Robert McGinnis, vice president of policy for the conservative Family Research Council, in *Christianity Today*, said that the U.S. would be justified attacking Iraq only if there were irrefutable evidence linking it to terrorism and the production of weapons of mass destruction for imminent use.

Dr. Land declared in an article released by the Baptist Press that military action would be justified under the ethical standards of Just War Theory because "Saddam Hussein is developing at breakneck speed weapons of mass destruction he plans to use against America and her allies." He stated that, "there is a direct line from those who attacked the U.S. [on Sept. 11] back to the nation of Iraq" (McMullen, 2002).

The IRD "stood tall" with Dr. Land (McMullen, 2002). In the process, Diane Knippers made the statement that comments made by two United Methodist leaders critical of the war on Iraq—Mr. Jim Winkler, General Secretary of the General Board of Church and Society and the Rev. Bob Edgar, General Secretary of the National Council of Churches—should be disregarded. The Lakeland Ledger newspaper in Florida quoted Ms. Knippers as saying "These church officials cannot be relied upon to contribute intelligently to the debate over war with Iraq, their vision of the world is largely divorced from historic Christian teachings about the use of force . . . "(McMullen, 2002). Our Lord Jesus Christ, whose views toward violence were nothing but disapproving, might consider that an odd point of view! In any event, the Florida newspaper found her opinion reprehensible: "Trying to silence duly elected religious leaders in a matter this momentous is odd indeed for someone who presides over an organization with religion and democracy in its title. Knippers' comments were neither religiously charitable nor democratic. It is difficult to see the views of Land, Knippers, and other like-minded individuals as anything other than a veneer of religious reasoning in the service of an undiluted nationalism" (McMullen, 2002).

Ms. Knippers also supports those who oppose hate crime laws. On August 10,1996, she released a letter in the name of IRD to the media accusing the National Council of Churches (NCC) of "perpetrating a hoax" regarding the well publicized 1995-1996 African-American church arsons across America (United Methodist News Service, 1996). Ms. Knippers accused the NCC of nefarious conduct, declaring that the 53-year-old ecumenical group had "exaggerated the church burning phenomenon to promote a radical agenda" and that its officials "jawboned" the church burning issue into a national crisis. Ms. Knippers claimed that the NCC had created the church arson story "absent evidence that black churches burn more frequently than white churches to raise money for its leftist political agenda" (UM News Service, 1996).

The NCC responded with facts. It made the point that arson and vandalism at African-American and multi-racial churches had "increased dramatically and persistently over the past 18 to 30 months." The Rev. Joan Brown Campbell, the NCC's chief executive at the time, noted that "more than 60 African-American and multiracial churches were burned between January 1, 1995, and June 30, 1996, more than in the previous five years combined." Dr. Campbell wrote that "while approximately the same number of black and white churches have been burned since 1995, black churches are burning in proportion to their number at four times the rate of white churches" (UM News Service, 1996).

FBI data support the NCC's assertions (Infoplease, 2000). The chief reason for hate crimes is racial bias, with African-Americans at the greatest risk. In 2000, of the 8,063 such crimes reported to the FBI, 54 percent (4,337) were race related, two-thirds of which targeted African-Americans. The types of crimes committed against African-Americans included bombing and vandalizing churches, burning crosses on home lawns, and murder. Among other racially-motivated crimes reported, about 20 percent were committed against European-Americans (Infoplease, 2000).

BUT MS. KNIPPERS WAS UNDETERRED. She expressed bizarre beliefs to the Wall Street Journal on August 9, 1996, charging the NCC with using church-arson "to justify its thesis that America is on the verge of a race war." According to the United Methodist News Service, she went further, claiming that the NCC had misrepresented the church burning issue "to smear... conservative Christians as racists." Hello? Was she suggesting that members of the Ku Klux Klan are merely persecuted conservative Christians?

In some ways, as outrageous as such declarations are, they are consistent with Ms. Knippers' stated convictions in other respects. The IRD has always worked hard for the political agenda of the right-wing. Ms. Knippers' highly vocal and vigorous opposition to hate-crime laws is just one example (Jones, 2000). She and her staff of eight are all European-American as are the 23 members of the IRD Board of Directors and all 20 members of the UM Action steering committee. Perhaps the IRD's position on hate crimes would be more sensitive if there were a few African-Americans in its organization.

At the same time the IRD is not above using hate language to attack United Methodists and others. Dave Berg, who has identified himself as a "segment producer" for the "Tonight Show with Jay Leno," wrote a commentary for IRD posted on its Web site on May 9, 2003 (Berg, 2003). In this column, after he announced that "the war in Iraq is coming to a victorious close," he attacked "the godless army of America's mainstream Protestant leaders" who "worship at the altar of the United Nations" and "gave aid and comfort" to our enemies. He named Jim Winker, General Secretary of the United Methodist General Board of Church and Society, Bishop Clifton Ives of West Virginia, and Bishop William Dew of Arizona, among his targets. He then directed towards these United Methodist leaders, hateful accusations. He said these respected men of God have "hatred for President Bush and for

America itself" (Berg, 2003).

One aspect of this attack group that merits note is that five of the 23 board members of the IRD are conservative Roman Catholics: Father Richard John Neuhaus, Michael Novak, Robert P. George, George Weigel, and Mary Ellen Bork (wife of Judge Robert Bork). One wonders: What are they doing working on a board and contributing to a group whose central aim is to undermine the witness of Protestant churches (Institute on Religion and Democracy, 2001a)?

Even after 20 years of bashing, however, there appears to be little grassroots support for IRD within the UMC. In a fundraising letter dated November 5, 1999, signed by Mark Tooley as Executive Director of UM Action and David Stanley as Chairman, they stated "We rely entirely upon the generosity of United Methodists like you. Over 8,000 individual United Methodists are now supporting our ministry, with an average donation of $30" (Stanley & Tooley, 1999). In an October of 2002 interview with the United Methodist Reporter, Mr. Tooley said that "The IRD operates on $1 million annually, about $400,000 of which is from 3,500 donors and goes to UM Action (Smith, 2002). On July 30, 2003, on the IRD Web site, Mr. Tooley said "The annual IRD budget is about $1 million a year, about a third of which goes to our United Methodist program. Half of IRD's budget comes from foundation support, while the other half comes from individual donors. IRD's United Methodist program relies mostly on small donors, of whom we have about 3,000. Their average gift is about $30" (Tooley, 2003).

Using IRD's own numbers, their donor base has dropped from 8000 to 3000, a 62.5 percent loss in less than four years, despite having sent out hundreds of thousands of unsolicited pieces of mail each year. Moreover, Mr. Tooley claims that his annual budget is now about $333,000, half of which he says comes from 3000 donors with an average contribution of $30. The numbers just do not add up!

The truth is that without wealthy right-wing patrons, the IRD would be quickly out of business. Much of the IRD's behavior would simply be dismissed as bad manners by people with poor social skills except that the IRD is well funded by wealthy non-United Methodist backers whose social agendas are at odds with the historical witness of the church. If

Scaife, Ahmanson, Olin, Coors, Bradley and their ilk are successful in disrupting the moral leadership of the UMC and other mainline Christian churches, they will have muted America's social conscience and significantly diminished its capacity for responsible civic discourse. At risk are the soul of the church and the nation.

REFERENCES

Berg, D. (2003). "Commentary: Anti-war protestants. Institute on Religion and Democracy." Retrieved on September 30, 2003, from http://www.ird-renew.org/news/news.cfm.

Bowdon, B.A. (2001, Sept. 21) "Jesus' promises are not pabulum, and they are not baloney!" Oklahoma Conference Communications, 4(16). Retrieved on October 14, 2003, from http://www.okumc.org/contact/2001/ 092101/jesus.html.

Brown, J. (2003). "Methodist theologian offers hope for evangelical UM churches on property issue." *Gospel Café, Inc.* Retrieved on November 24, 2003 from www.gospelcafe.org.

Case, R (2002). "It's time we talk about 'amiable separation'." *The New Zion's Herald*, 177(6), 21.

Case, R.B. (2003). "Do renewal groups threaten the health of United Methodism?" *Good News Magazine*. Retrieved on December 2, 2003, from www.goodnewsmag.org.

Clark, D.G. (1999). "Clark opposes proposed Iowa constitutional amendment." Letter published as an op-ed in the *Muscatine Journal*, June 25, 1999. Retrieved on December 9, 2003, from http://www.muscanet.com/~dclark/published/journal-oped699.html.

Cooperman, A. (2003). "Conservatives funding opposition, priest says: Groups insist donors don't set agenda." *Washington Post*, Friday, October 24.

Goodenough, P. (2003, May). "Bush urged to reject calls for softer line with North Korea." CNSNews.com. Retrieved from http://www.cnsnews.com/ images/ International.gif.

Hartmann, T. (February 25, 2003). "Healthcare reveals real "conservative" agenda - drown democracy in a bathtub." Common Dreams Center: Breaking News & Views for the Progressive Community. *Common Dreams*. Retrieved on November 20, 2003 from www.commondreams.org.

Henderson, B. (2003). The United Methodist ministerial education fund. Retrieved on December 2, 2003, from http://www.NWHillsUMC.org.

Hout, M., Greely, A., & Wilde, M. J. (2001). "The demographic imperative in religious change in the United States." *American Journal of Sociology*, 107(2), 468-500.

Howell, L. (1995). "Funding the war of ideas: A report to the United Church Board for Homeland Ministries." Cleveland, OH: United Church Board for Homeland Ministries

Howell, L. (2003). *United Methodism@ Risk: A Wake-up Call*. Kingston, NY: Information Project for United Methodists.

Infoplease. (2000). Summary of hate crime statistics. (2000). Retrieved March 29, 2002, from www.infoplease.com/ipa/A0004885.html.

Information Project for United Methodists. (2003). *United Methodism@Risk: A Wake-up Call*, http://www.ipum.org/images/riskbookcover.jpgby Leon Howell: A story: You've got to be kidding. Information Project for United Methodists. Retrieved on October 14, 2003, from http://www.ipum.org/1marykraus.html.

Institute on Religion and Democracy. (2001a). "Institute on religion and democracy's reforming America's churches project: 2001-2004, executive summary." Retrieved on September 30, 2003 from www.4religious-right.info/internal_ document_ird.html.

Institute on Religion and Democracy. (2001b). "Church leaders rally against land mines." Institute on Religion and Democracy. Retrieved on October 6, 2003, from http://www.ird-renew.org/About/About.cfm.

Institute on Religion and Democracy. (2001c). Methodist agency endorses reinstatement of funding for overseas abortion. Institute on Religion and Democracy. Retrieved on October 3, 2003, from http://www.ird-renew.org/About/About.cfm.

Interfaith Alliance. (2003). Board of Directors. The Interfaith Alliance. Retrieved on October 3, 2003, from www.interfaithalliance.org/About/AboutList.cfm.

Interfaith Coalition for Environmental Stewardship. Religion and the environment. Retrieved on September 26, 2003, from http://www.stewards.net/About.htm.

Jones, D. (2000). "Hate crime petitions gain wide support. Response." Retrieved on September 30, 2003 from http://gbgm-umc.org/Response/articles/hatecrimepets.html.

Kaiser, R.G., & Chinoy, I. (1999). Scaife: Funding father of the right. Retrieved on September 4, 2003, from www.washingtonpost.com/wp-srv/politics/special/clinto/stories/scaifemain.

Kennedy, J.F. (1999). "Who's afraid of Richard Mellon Scaife?" (JFK, Jr. Interviews Richard Mellon Scaife). *George Magazine*. Retrieved September 4, 2003, from http://www.freerepublic.com/forum/a3693c60d6e04.htm%0DAbridged%20from%20.

McIntyre, D. (2001, Aug. 29). "A reply to a letter of concern about the faith we sing." *The Faith We Sing*. Retrieved on October 14, 2003, from www.gbod.org/worship/events/ faithsing/letterreply.html.

McMullen, C. (2002). "Cries of the hawk not silenced: beliefs." Lakeland, FL: Lakeland Ledger Publishing.

Media Transparency. (2003). "The money behind the media." Institute on Religion and Democracy, Inc. Retrieved from http://www.mediatransparency.org/search_results/info_on_any_recipient.php?174.

Nation, (2003, December 22). "What Recovery?" 277(21), 4-5.

National Committee for Responsive Philanthropy. (1997). Conservative foundations prevail in shaping public policies: New report documents public policy impact of 12 core foundations. Retrieved on September 4, 2003, from www.ncrp.org/reports/moving.htm.

National Taxpayers Union. (2003). "Upper brackets: The right's tax cut boosters." Retrieved on November 20, 2003 from www.nta.org

Neas, R.G. (2003, March 27). "Upper brackets: The right's tax cut boosters." People for the American Way. Retrieved on October 14, 2003, from http://www.pfaw.org/pfaw/general/ default.aspx.

Neuhaus, R.J. (1997, August/September). "In the Beauty of Holiness." The Public Square. Retrieved September 26, 2003, from http://www.firstthings.com/ ftissues/ ft9708/public.html

Olsen, W. (1998). "Invitation to a stoning: Getting cozy with theocrats." Reason. Retrieved on December 1, 2003 from www.reason.com/9811/col.olson.shtml.

PBS. (2003). "The strategy: Shield. . . or sword?" PBS. Retrieved on December 9, 2003, from www.pbs.org/wgbh.

Public Eye. (1989). Group watch: Institute on Religion and Democracy. Retrieved on September 4, 2003, from http://www.publiceye.org/ research/Group_Watch/Entries-76.htm.

Public Eye. (2003). Environment. The Public Eye. Retrieved from http://www.publiceye.org/magazine/v15n1/State_of_Christian_Rt-09.htm.

Right Wing Organizations (2003). Concerned women for America. Retrieved on November 21, 2003, from www.cwfa.org.

Robinson, B. A. (2002). "Christian reconstructionism, dominion theology, and theonomy." Ontario Consultants on Religious Tolerance. Retrieved on November 14, 2003 from www.religioustolerance.org.

Rothmyer, K. (2000). The man behind the mask. Retrieved on September 4, 2003, from Salon, http://www.salon.com/news/1998/04/07news.html.

Sider, R., & Ball, J. (2002). A response to Mark Tooley. Institute on Religion and Democracy. Retrieved on October 2, 2003, from http://www.ird-renew.org.

Smith, S. (2002). "New group challenges UMC's 'right wing.' " Reporter Interactive. Retrieved September 26, 2003 from http://www.reporterinteractive. org/news/100202/project.htm

Smithson, W.C. (2003). "Welcome. Iowa ethics & campaign disclosure board." Retrieved on November 26, 2003, from www.state.ia.us/government/iecdb.

Stanley, D., & Tooley, M. (1999). Letter to United Methodists. United Methodist Action. Retrieved on September 30, 2003, from http://www.ucmpage.org/umaction/ gc200letter.htm

Stone, R.H. (2001). *John Wesley's Life and Ethics.* Nashville: Abingdon Press.

Taylor, J.H. (2003). American Anglican council and institute for religion and democracy. Do Justice: A series of essays towards General Convention in 2003. Retrieved on December 1, 2003, from http://www.rci.rutgers.edu/~lcrew/dojustice.html.

Tooley, M. (2001a). "A Methodist president and his bishops." Good News. Retrieved on October 3, 2003, from www.goodnewsmag.org/news/bushbish_03_14_01.html.

Tooley, M. (2001b). "Church leaders and tax collectors." Institute on Religion and Democracy. Retrieved on October 2, 2003.

Tooley, M. (2001c). "Tax cuts statement 1: When your church opposes tax cuts, does it speak for you?" Methodist Laity Reform Movement, Institute on Religion and Democracy. Retrieved on October 2, 2003 from http://www.mreform.org/taxcuts_statement_1htm=ird++%22mark++tooley

Tooley, M. (2002). "What would Jesus drive?" Institute on Religion and Democracy. Retrieved on October 2, 2003, http://www.ird-renew.org.

Tooley, M. (2003, July 30). "What is the fight really about?" Institute on Religion and Democracy. Retrieved on October 6, 2003, from http://www.ird-renew.org/About/About.cfm.

Tooley, M. (2003). Report to UM Action board of directors. UM Action News. Retrieved on December 2, 2003, from www.ird.org.

UM Action. (2000). 2000 news reports: UM action briefing. Institute for Religion and Democracy. Retrieved on October 8, 2003, from http://www.ucmpage.org/umaction/ news00.htm.

UMAction. (2003). "Reform agenda: A reform agenda for United Methodists." The Institute on Religion and Democracy. Retrieved on December 1, 2003, from www.ird.org.

United Methodist News Service. (1996). NCC Responds to IRD. Worldwide Faith News. Retrieved on October 2, 2003, from http://www.wfn.org/1996/08/msg00041.html.

United Methodists Affirming Christ's Teachings in our Nation (2003). Links to the writings of Mark Tooley. United Methodists Affirming Christ's Teachings in our Nation. Retrieved on October 8, 2003, from http://umaction.org/ index.htm.

Willimon, W. (2001). "Under fire." *Christian Century*. Retrieved on October 3, 2003, from http://www.christiancentury.org.

Willimon, W. (2003). Personal Communication, September 14, 2003.

Yepsen, D. (May 4, 2003). Yepsen: Give all our grandchildren a brighter future - in Iowa. *Des Moines Register*. Retrieved on November 20, 2003 from www.desmoinesregester.com

Zion's Herald (2003) "The rich grow richer." *Zion Herald*,177(6), 22.

authOrs
authors
AUTHORS
authOrs
Authors
Authors
authors

INDEX OF AUTHORS

Abu-Rabi', Ibrahim M., 127
Ambrogi, Thomas, 162
Armstrong, James, 31
Astle, Cynthia B., 36, 147, 181
Bageant, Joe, 219
Benner, Betty, 17
Blackburn, Steven, 87
Campbell, Scott, 101, 111, 118
Dale, Beverly, 46
Denson, John Lane, 72
Fassett, Thom White Wolf, 53
Gallen, Thomas J., xi
Gould, William B., 214
Gracey, Colin B., 12
Gray, Richard M., 136
Hadsell, Heidi, 82
Hazo, Samuel, 130
Herbert, Mary Kennan, 134
Landau, Yehezkel, 104
Latham, Jennifer, 152
Lovelace, John, 225
MacDonald, G. Jeffrey, 25
Mount, Eric, 3

Neville, Robert Cummings, 167
Randall, Lyman, 133, 184
Rankin, Stephen W., 60
Rieger, Joerg, 122
Robertson, Anne, 141
Schaper, Donna, 23, 149
Schuster, Charles, 222
Seibert, Nicole, 243
Shasha, David, 200
Shetterly, Robert, 42
Shoemaker, Jan, 174
Sidorak, Stephen J., 187
Slater, Glen, 206
Slattery, Dennis Patrick, 210
Smith, Jane I., 95
Swecker, Stephen, xviii, 229-240
Tremba, Randall, 67
Weaver, Andrew J., 243
Weems, Lovett H., 157
Winn, John, 195
Wogaman, J. Philip, 77, 92, 115
Wren, Brian, 129

Additional copies of this book can
be purchased at Amazon.com.

•

Discounts for 5 or more copies are available.
To request a quote, drop a line
to **info@ridergreen.com.**

•

Standard commercial and institutional
discounts are available upon request
at **info@ridergreen.com.**

•

For further information, contact
Rider Green Book Publishers
P.O. Box 488
North Berwick ME 03906
(207) 457-5088

Made in the USA
Charleston, SC
04 December 2014